MW00682369

meat

meat

MURDOCH BOOKS

contents

meaty meals	7
beef	8
lamb	74
pork	138
index	196

meaty meals

Meat lovers rejoice! Assembled together in this exciting volume are the most tantalizing, mouth-watering and downright yummiest recipes ever for beef, veal, lamb and pork. Whether you crave a succulent, tender steak grilled to utter perfection, slices of roast carved from a crusty, juicy joint or meaty morsels simmered to rich tenderness in a nourishing stew or soup, your every meaty whim will be indulged when you cook from these pages. All the firm favourites are well represented, and there are new, updated spins on classic combinations.

Lovers of global flavours haven't been neglected either. Trawling the vast international treasury of meat dishes has yielded delicious fare from Japan, India, China and the Middle East, among others. Adventurous cooks can easily conjure global classics, as even supermarkets stock most of the spices, herbs and other ethnic ingredients required.

Meat, as well as being universally popular, is also surprisingly versatile — you'll be amazed at the range of meat-based dishes it is possible to make. Yes, meat can be hearty — what would be the purpose of winter, after all, without the soothing comfort of hearty meat stews? But meat can also take on far lighter guises too, and appears in salads, sandwiches, stir-fries and light soups. Whether served hot or cold, on the bone or off, plain or embellished with garnishes and sauce, meat is delicious. In fact, the only thing that meat cookery should never be is boring and, thanks to this book, it will never be that again.

beef

Oxtail and vegetable soup

2 kg (4 lb 8 oz) oxtails, trimmed
2 tablespoons oil
2 onions, finely chopped
1 leek, white part only, finely
  chopped
2 carrots, diced
1 celery stalk, diced
2 garlic cloves, crushed
2 bay leaves
2 tablespoons tomato paste
  (concentrated purée)
1 thyme sprig

2 flat-leaf (Italian) parsley sprigs
3.5 litres (122 fl oz/14 cups)
  chicken stock
375 ml (13 fl oz/1½ cups) stout
2 tomatoes, seeded and diced
100 g (3½ oz) cauliflower florets
100 g (3½ oz) green beans,
  trimmed
100 g (3½ oz) broccoli florets
100 g (3½ oz) asparagus,
  trimmed and cut into 3 cm
  (1¼ inch) lengths

Preheat the oven to 200°C (400°F/Gas 6). Place the oxtails in a roasting tin and roast, turning occasionally, for 1 hour, or until dark golden. Leave to cool.

Heat the oil in a large saucepan over medium heat and cook the onion, leek, carrot and celery for 3–4 minutes, or until soft. Stir in the garlic, bay leaves and tomato paste, then add the oxtails, thyme and parsley. Pour in the stock and bring to the boil over high heat. Reduce the heat and simmer for 3 hours, or until the oxtails are tender and the meat falls off the bone. Skim off any scum that rises to the surface and remove the bay leaves. Lift the oxtails out of the pan and allow to cool slightly.

Take the meat off the bones and discard any fat or sinew. Roughly chop the meat and add it to the pan along with the stout, tomato and 500 ml (17 fl oz/2 cups) water. Bring to the boil, then add the vegetables and simmer for 5 minutes, or until the vegetables are tender. Season before ladling into bowls to serve.

SERVES 4

Fajitas

185 ml (6 fl oz/¾ cup) olive oil
2 tablespoons lime juice
4 garlic cloves, chopped
3 red chillies, chopped
2 tablespoons tequila (optional)
1 kg (2 lb 4 oz) rump steak, trimmed and
    thinly sliced into strips
1 red capsicum (pepper), thinly sliced
1 yellow capsicum (pepper), thinly sliced
1 red onion, thinly sliced
8 flour tortillas
guacamole, shredded lettuce, diced tomato
    and sour cream, to serve

Combine the oil, lime juice, garlic, chilli, tequila (if using) and some pepper in a
large non-metallic bowl. Add the steak and coat the strips in the marinade. Cover
and marinate in the fridge for several hours, or overnight if time permits.

Drain the meat and toss it with the capsicum and onion. Around the time that you
want to eat, wrap the tortillas in foil and warm them in a 150°C (300°F/Gas 2) oven
for about 5 minutes.

Cook the meat and vegetables in batches in a sizzling hot heavy-based frying pan until
cooked, then scoop onto a serving plate and sit in the middle of the table with the
tortillas, guacamole, shredded lettuce, diced tomato and sour cream. Let everyone
assemble their own fajita.

SERVES 4

Beef, stout and potato pie

2 tablespoons olive oil
1.25 kg (2 lb 12 oz) chuck steak, trimmed and cut into 3 cm (1¼ inch) cubes
2 onions, sliced
2 bacon slices, roughly chopped
4 garlic cloves, crushed
2 tablespoons plain (all-purpose) flour
435 ml (15¼ fl oz/1¾ cups) stout
375 ml (13 fl oz/1½ cups) beef stock
1½ tablespoons chopped thyme
2 large all-purpose potatoes, thinly sliced
olive oil, for brushing

Heat 1 tablespoon of the oil over high heat in a large heavy-based flameproof casserole dish, add the beef in batches and cook, turning occasionally, for 5 minutes, or until the meat is nicely coloured. Remove from the dish. Reduce the heat to low, add the remaining oil to the dish, then cook the onion and bacon for 10 minutes, stirring occasionally. Add the garlic and cook for another minute. Return the beef to the dish.

Sprinkle the flour over the beef, cook for a minute, stirring, then gradually add the stout, stirring constantly. Pour in the stock, increase the heat to medium–high and bring to the boil. Stir in the thyme, season, then reduce the heat and simmer for 2 hours, or until the beef is tender and the mixture has thickened.

Preheat the oven to 200°C (400°F/Gas 6). Lightly grease a 1.25 litre (44 fl oz/5 cup) ovenproof dish and pour in the beef mixture. Arrange potato slices in a single overlapping layer over the top to cover the meat. Brush the top with olive oil and sprinkle with salt. Bake for 30–40 minutes, or until the potato is golden. Serve with steamed vegetables or salad.

SERVES 6

Silverside with parsley sauce

1.5 kg (3 lb 5 oz) corned beef
    (silverside)
1 teaspoon black peppercorns
5 cloves
2 bay leaves, torn
2 tablespoons soft brown sugar

Parsley sauce
50 g (1¾ oz) butter
1½ tablespoons plain
    (all-purpose) flour
400 ml (14 fl oz) milk
125 ml (4 fl oz/½ cup) beef stock
2 tablespoons chopped parsley

Soak the corned beef in cold water for 45 minutes, changing the water 3–4 times. This helps eliminate some of the salty flavour.

Lift the beef out of the water and put it in a large heavy-based saucepan with the peppercorns, cloves, bay leaves, brown sugar and enough cold water to just cover it. Bring to the boil, then reduce the heat to very low and simmer for 1½–1¾ hours. Turn the meat over every 30 minutes and keep an eye on the water level — you'll probably need to add some more. You don't want the water to boil or the meat will become tough, so use a heat diffuser mat if you need to. Remove the meat from the pan and let it rest for 15 minutes.

To make the parsley sauce, melt the butter in a saucepan over medium heat, then stir in the flour and keep stirring for 1 minute. Take the pan off the heat and pour in the milk and stock, whisking until smooth. Return the pan to the heat and cook, whisking constantly, until the sauce boils and thickens. Reduce the heat and simmer for 2 minutes more before stirring in the parsley and a little salt and pepper. Serve over slices of silverside with steamed vegetables.

SERVES 6

Barbecued rosemary and red wine steaks with vegetables

12 small new potatoes
3 tablespoons olive oil
1 tablespoon finely chopped
    rosemary
6 garlic cloves, sliced
sea salt flakes

4 large, thick field mushrooms
12 asparagus spears, trimmed
250 ml (9 fl oz/1 cup) red wine
4 x 260 g (9¼ oz) scotch fillet
    (rib-eye) steaks

Heat a barbecue chargrill plate or flat plate to high direct heat. Toss the potatoes with 1 tablespoon of the oil, half the rosemary and half the garlic and season with the sea salt flakes. Divide the potatoes among four large sheets of foil and wrap into neat packages, sealing firmly around the edges. Cook on the barbecue, turning frequently for 30–40 minutes, or until tender.

Meanwhile, brush the mushrooms and asparagus with a little of the remaining oil and set aside.

Combine the red wine and the remaining oil, rosemary and garlic in a non-metallic dish. Add a generous amount of black pepper. Add the steaks and coat them in the marinade. Cover and marinate for 25 minutes, then drain.

Cook the steaks and mushrooms on the barbecue for 4 minutes on each side, or until cooked to your liking (this will depend on the thickness of the steak). Transfer both to a plate, cover lightly and allow to rest. Add the asparagus to the barbecue and cook, turning regularly, for about 2 minutes, or until tender. Pierce the potatoes with a skewer to check for doneness. Season. Serve the steaks with the vegetables.

SERVES 4

Italian beef casserole with polenta dumplings

2 tablespoons olive oil
1 onion, sliced
2 garlic cloves, crushed
1 tablespoon plain (all-purpose) flour
1 kg (2 lb 4 oz) chuck steak, trimmed and cut into 3 cm (1¼ inch) cubes
375 ml (13 fl oz/1½ cups) beef stock

1 tablespoon chopped oregano
2 x 400 g (14 oz) tins chopped tomatoes
2 red capsicums (peppers), roasted, peeled and cut into strips
100 g (3½ oz/⅔ cup) instant polenta
4 tablespoons ready-made pesto

Preheat the oven to 150°C (300°F/Gas 2). Heat the oil in a 4 litre (140 fl oz/16 cup) flameproof casserole dish, add the onion and garlic and cook over medium heat for 8 minutes, or until soft but not browned. Sprinkle the flour over the top and stir well. Add the beef, stock, oregano, tomato and capsicum, season and simmer for 15 minutes, then bake, covered, for 1½ hours.

Pour 300 ml (10½ fl oz) water into a saucepan, bring to the boil, then reduce the heat and simmer. Pour in the polenta in a thin stream, season and cook, stirring, for 2 minutes, or until it thickens and comes away from the side of the pan. Remove the pan from the heat and allow to cool.

Shape the cooled polenta into 12 round dumplings, place on top of the casserole and bake, covered, for 1 hour, then remove the lid and cook for another 20–30 minutes. Serve in bowls with a dollop of the pesto on top.

SERVES 4–6

Chinese beef and asparagus with oyster sauce

1 tablespoon light soy sauce
½ teaspoon sesame oil
1 tablespoon Chinese rice wine
500 g (1 lb 2 oz) lean beef fillet,
  thinly sliced across the grain
2½ tablespoons vegetable oil
200 g (7 oz) thin asparagus,
  trimmed and cut into thirds
  on the diagonal

3 garlic cloves, crushed
2 teaspoons julienned fresh
  ginger
3 tablespoons chicken stock
2–3 tablespoons oyster sauce

Combine the soy sauce, sesame oil and 2 teaspoons of the rice wine in a large non-metallic bowl. Add the beef and coat in the marinade. Cover and marinate for at least 15 minutes.

Heat a wok to very hot, add 1 tablespoon of the vegetable oil and swirl to coat the side. When the oil is hot but not smoking, add the asparagus and stir-fry for 1–2 minutes. Remove from the wok.

Add another tablespoon of oil to the wok and add the beef in two batches, stir-frying each batch for 1–2 minutes, or until cooked. Remove from the wok.

Add the remaining oil to the wok and, when hot, add the garlic and ginger and stir-fry for 1 minute, or until fragrant. Pour the stock, oyster sauce and remaining rice wine into the wok, bring to the boil and boil rapidly for 1–2 minutes, or until the sauce is slightly reduced. Return the beef and asparagus to the wok and stir-fry for a further minute, or until heated through and coated in the sauce. Serve immediately with steamed rice.

SERVES 4

Steak with green peppercorn sauce

4 x 200 g (7 oz) fillet steaks
30 g (1 oz) butter
2 teaspoons oil
250 ml (9 fl oz/1 cup) beef stock
185 ml (6 fl oz/¾ cup) cream
2 teaspoons cornflour (cornstarch)
2 tablespoons green peppercorns in brine,
    rinsed and drained
2 tablespoons brandy

Bash the steaks with a meat mallet to 1.5 cm (⅝ inch) thick, then nick the edges of the steaks to prevent them from curling when they are cooking.

Heat the butter and oil in a large heavy-based frying pan over high heat. Fry the steaks for 2–4 minutes on each side, or until cooked to your liking. Transfer to a serving plate and cover with foil.

Add the stock to the pan juices and stir over low heat until boiling. Combine the cream and cornflour, then pour the mixture into the pan and stir constantly for a few minutes until the sauce becomes smooth and thick. Add the peppercorns and brandy and boil for 1 more minute before taking the pan off the heat. Spoon the sauce over the steaks and serve with fries.

SERVES 4

Coconut beef curry on turmeric rice

2 tablespoons oil
1 large onion, sliced
2 tablespoons vindaloo curry paste
1 kg (2 lb 4 oz) chuck steak, trimmed and
    cut into 3 cm (1¼ inch) cubes
250 ml (9 fl oz/1 cup) beef stock
200 ml (7 fl oz) coconut cream
250 g (9 oz/1¼ cups) basmati rice
¾ teaspoon ground turmeric

Heat the oil in a large saucepan over medium–high heat. Add the onion and cook for 2–3 minutes, or until starting to soften. Add the curry paste and stir for 1 minute, or until fragrant. Add the steak and brown evenly for about 5 minutes.

Pour in the stock and bring to the boil. Reduce the heat to very low and simmer, covered, for 1 hour, or until the meat is tender. Uncover and cook for 15 minutes to reduce the sauce.

Add the coconut cream, return to the boil, then simmer over low heat for 15–20 minutes, or until the beef is tender and the sauce has reduced.

About 25 minutes before the beef is ready, rinse the rice and put it in a large saucepan. Add the turmeric and 435 ml (15¼ fl oz/1¾ cups) water and bring to the boil. Reduce the heat to very low, then cook, covered, for 10 minutes. Remove from the heat and leave to stand, covered, for 10 minutes. Divide the rice among four wide serving bowls and top with the beef curry.

SERVES 4

Beef and beet borscht

2 tablespoons olive oil
1 onion, chopped
2 garlic cloves, crushed
500 g (1 lb 2 oz) chuck steak,
   trimmed and cut into 2 cm
   (¾ inch) cubes
1 litre (35 fl oz/4 cups) beef stock
2 small beetroot (beets)
200 g (7 oz) tinned chopped
   tomatoes

1 carrot, diced
2 all-purpose potatoes, diced
190 g (6¾ oz/2½ cups) finely
   shredded cabbage
2 teaspoons lemon juice
2 teaspoons sugar
2 tablespoons chopped flat-leaf
   (Italian) parsley
2 tablespoons chopped dill
4 tablespoons sour cream

Preheat the oven to 200°C (400°F/Gas 6). Heat the oil in a large saucepan and cook the onion and garlic over medium heat for 3–5 minutes. Add the beef, stock and 1 litre (35 fl oz/4 cups) water, then bring to the boil. Reduce the heat and simmer, covered, for 1¼ hours, or until the meat is tender. Remove the meat.

Trim the beetroot just above the end of the leaf stalks. Wrap in foil and bake for 30–40 minutes, or until tender. Unwrap and leave to cool.

Return the stock to the boil and add the tomato, carrot and potato, and season with salt. Cook over medium heat for 10 minutes. Add the cabbage and cook for 5 minutes. Peel and dice the beetroot. Return the meat to the pan and add the beetroot, lemon juice, sugar and 1½ tablespoons each of parsley and dill. Cook for 2 minutes, or until heated through. Season to taste. Remove from the heat and leave for 10 minutes. Serve in bowls with a dollop of sour cream on top and a sprinkling of the remaining dill and parsley.

SERVES 4

Fillet steak with mixed mushrooms

1 tablespoon oil
60 g (2¼ oz) butter
4 x 165 g (5¾ oz) scotch fillet (rib-eye) steaks,
    2.5 cm (1 inch) thick
3 garlic cloves, finely chopped
250 g (9 oz) mixed mushrooms
2 teaspoons chopped thyme
125 ml (4 fl oz/½ cup) dry sherry

Melt the oil and 20 g (¾ oz) of the butter in a large frying pan. Cook the steaks for 3–4 minutes on each side for medium–rare, or until cooked to your liking. Remove from the pan, cover with foil and rest.

Melt another 20 g (¾ oz) of the butter in the pan over medium heat. Add the garlic and mushrooms and season to taste. Cook for 3–4 minutes, or until the mushrooms have softened. Stir in the thyme. Remove from the pan.

Add the sherry and any juices from the rested meat to the pan and stir to scrape up any sediment from the base. Bring to the boil, then reduce the heat and simmer for 2–3 minutes, or until reduced to 4 tablespoons and thickened slightly. Whisk in the remaining butter in small amounts, until glossy.

To serve, put the steaks on four serving plates, top with the mushrooms and spoon the sauce over the top. Serve with steamed greens.

SERVES 4

Veal scaloppine with sage

600 g (1 lb 5 oz) small new potatoes, halved
4 tablespoons olive oil
8 x 80 g (2¾ oz) veal escalopes
4 pancetta slices, halved
8 sage leaves
250 ml (9 fl oz/1 cup) dry Marsala

Preheat the oven to 200°C (400°F/Gas 6). Boil the potatoes for 10 minutes. Drain, then transfer to a baking tray with 2 tablespoons of the olive oil. Toss well and bake for 40–50 minutes, or until crisp.

Place the veal escalopes between two sheets of baking paper and pound with a meat mallet or rolling pin until they are 5 mm (¼ inch) thick. Press a piece of pancetta and a sage leaf onto each veal escalope, then skewer in place with a toothpick. Season with salt and freshly ground black pepper.

Heat the remaining oil in a large heavy-based frying pan. Cook the veal (in batches if necessary), pancetta side down, for 1–2 minutes, then turn over and cook for 1 minute. Remove from the pan and keep warm. Add the Marsala to the pan and cook for 4–5 minutes, or until syrupy and reduced by half. Return the scaloppine to the pan and toss lightly in the sauce until warmed through.

Remove the toothpicks and divide the scaloppine among serving plates. Drizzle any pan juices on top. Serve with the potatoes and some steamed asparagus.

SERVES 4

Beef bourguignon

1 kg (2 lb 4 oz) chuck steak,
   trimmed and cut into 3 cm
   (1¼ inch) cubes
seasoned flour, to coat
2 tablespoons oil
200 g (7 oz) bacon, chopped
30 g (1 oz) butter
150 g (5½ oz) baby onions
3 garlic cloves, finely chopped
1 leek, white part only, sliced
250 g (9 oz) button mushrooms

2 carrots, diced
3 tablespoons tomato paste
   (concentrated purée)
500 ml (17 fl oz/2 cups) red wine
500 ml (17 fl oz/2 cups) beef
   stock
2 teaspoons chopped thyme
2 bay leaves
4 tablespoons finely chopped
   flat-leaf (Italian) parsley

Toss the meat in the flour to coat. Shake off any excess. Heat the oil in a large saucepan, add the bacon and cook over medium heat for 3–4 minutes, or until lightly browned. Remove from the pan. Add the beef in small batches and cook for 3–4 minutes, or until starting to brown. Remove from the pan.

Melt the butter in the pan, add the onions, garlic and leek, and cook for 4–5 minutes, or until softened.

Return the beef and bacon to the pan, add the remaining ingredients, except the parsley, and stir well. Bring to the boil, then reduce the heat and simmer, covered, stirring occasionally, for 1 hour, then uncovered for 30 minutes, or until the meat is very tender and the sauce thickened. Remove the bay leaves and stir in the parsley. Serve with mashed potato.

SERVES 6

Eye fillet with blue cheese butter

100 g (3½ oz) butter, softened
2 garlic cloves, crushed
100 g (3½ oz) Blue Castello cheese
2 teaspoons finely shredded sage
1 kg (2 lb 4 oz) eye fillet (thick end), trimmed
1 tablespoon olive oil

To make the blue cheese butter, mash together the softened butter, garlic, cheese and sage until they are well combined. Form the mixture into a log and wrap it in baking paper, twisting the ends to seal. Refrigerate the butter until firm, then cut it into 5 mm (¼ inch) thick slices and leave it at room temperature until needed.

Heat a barbecue chargrill plate or flat plate to medium–high direct heat. Cut the beef into four thick, equal pieces and tie a piece of string around the edge of each so it will keep its shape during cooking. Brush both sides of each steak with the oil and season with black pepper. Cook on the barbecue for 6–7 minutes on each side for medium, or to your liking.

As soon as you take the steaks off the barbecue, cut off the string and top each steak with two slices of blue cheese butter. This is delicious served with a pear and walnut salad.

SERVES 4

NOTE: Any leftover butter can be wrapped in baking paper and foil, and frozen for up to 2 months. It is also delicious with chicken and pork.

Veal Parmigiana

3 tablespoons olive oil
1 garlic clove, crushed
pinch cayenne pepper
pinch caster (superfine) sugar
400 g (14 oz) tin chopped
   tomatoes
3 teaspoons chopped oregano
4 tablespoons plain
   (all-purpose) flour

2 eggs
60 g (2¼ oz/⅔ cup) dry
   breadcrumbs
4 large veal cutlets, well
   trimmed
100 g (3½ oz) mozzarella
   cheese, thinly sliced
4 tablespoons grated parmesan
   cheese

Preheat the oven to 190°C (375°F/Gas 5). To make the sauce, heat 1 tablespoon of the oil in a small saucepan over medium heat, add the garlic and cook for 30 seconds. Add the cayenne, sugar, tomato and half the oregano and cook, stirring occasionally, for 20 minutes, or until thickened. Season well.

Put the flour in a wide shallow bowl and season with salt and freshly ground black pepper. Beat the eggs with 2 tablespoons of water in another bowl. Mix the breadcrumbs with the remaining oregano in a third bowl and season.

Place the veal cutlets between two sheets of baking paper and pound with a meat mallet or rolling pin until they are 5 mm (¼ inch) thick, taking care not to tear the flesh from the bone. Coat in the seasoned flour, shaking off the excess, then dip both sides in the egg mixture and then coat in the breadcrumbs. Heat the remaining oil in a large frying pan. Add the cutlets in two batches and brown over medium–high heat for 2 minutes on each side. Transfer to a shallow roasting tin large enough to fit them side by side.

Spread the sauce over each cutlet. Cover with the mozzarella and sprinkle with the parmesan. Bake for 20 minutes, or until the cheese has melted and browned. Serve.

SERVES 4

Chinese beef and gai larn stir-fry

3 tablespoons oil
1 kg (2 lb 4 oz) fresh rice noodle
    rolls, cut into 2 cm (¾ inch)
    strips, separated
500 g (1 lb 2 oz) rump steak,
    trimmed and thinly sliced
1 onion, cut into wedges
4 garlic cloves, chopped

400 g (14 oz) Chinese broccoli
    (gai larn), cut into 3 cm
    (1¼ inch) lengths
1 tablespoon soy sauce
3 tablespoons kecap manis
1 small red chilli, chopped
125 ml (4 fl oz/½ cup) beef
    stock

Heat a wok to hot, add 2 tablespoons of the oil and swirl to coat the side. Add the noodles and stir-fry gently for 2 minutes. Remove from the wok.

Reheat the wok over high heat, add the remaining oil and swirl to coat. Add the beef in batches and cook for 3 minutes, or until it is browned. Remove from the wok. Add the onion and stir-fry for 1–2 minutes, then add the garlic and cook for a further 30 seconds.

Return all the beef to the wok and add the Chinese broccoli, soy sauce, kecap manis, chilli and beef stock, then cook over medium heat for 2–3 minutes. Divide the rice noodles among four large serving bowls and top with the beef mixture. Serve immediately.

SERVES 4

NOTE: The noodles may break up during cooking. This will not affect the flavour of the dish.

Mustard-crusted
scotch fillet with roast vegetables

16 French shallots
125 g (4½ oz/½ cup) wholegrain mustard
3 garlic cloves, crushed
1.25–1.5 kg (2 lb 12 oz–3 lb 5 oz) scotch fillet (rib-eye) roast
200 g (7 oz) parsnips, cut into 2 cm (¾ inch) chunks
400 g (14 oz) roasting potatoes, cut lengthways into wedges
200 g (7 oz) orange sweet potato, cut into wedges
4 tablespoons olive oil

Preheat the oven to 200°C (400°F/Gas 6). Peel four of the French shallots, slice into thick rings and arrange them in the centre of a large roasting tin.

Combine the mustard and garlic, and season well with salt and pepper. Rub the mixture over the surface of the beef, then place the beef on top of the sliced shallots. Toss the parsnip, potato, sweet potato, the remaining shallots, and 3 tablespoons of the oil together, then arrange around the beef. Drizzle the remaining oil over the beef and roast for 30 minutes.

Season and turn the vegetables — don't worry if some of the mustard mixes through. Roast for a further 30 minutes for a medium–rare result, or until cooked to your liking. Rest in a warm place for 10 minutes.

To serve, carve the beef and spoon the pan juices on the top. Serve with the roasted vegetables, whole shallots, and some steamed greens, if desired.

SERVES 4

Chinese beef in soy

4 tablespoons dark soy sauce
2 tablespoons honey
1 tablespoon rice vinegar
700 g (1 lb 9 oz) chuck steak,
    trimmed and cut into 2 cm
    (¾ inch) cubes
3 tablespoons oil
4 garlic cloves, chopped
8 spring onions (scallions), thinly
    sliced, plus extra, to garnish

1 tablespoon finely grated
    fresh ginger
2 star anise
½ teaspoon ground cloves
375 ml (13 fl oz/1½ cups) beef
    stock
125 ml (4 fl oz/½ cup) red wine

Combine the soy sauce, honey and vinegar in a large non-metallic bowl. Add the meat and coat it in the marinade. Cover and marinate in the fridge for 2 hours, or overnight if time permits. Drain, reserving the marinade, and pat the meat dry.

Heat 1 tablespoon of the oil in a saucepan over medium heat and brown the meat in three batches, for 3–4 minutes per batch — add another tablespoon of oil, if necessary. Remove the meat. Add the remaining oil and fry the garlic, spring onion, ginger, star anise and cloves for 1–2 minutes, or until fragrant.

Return all the meat to the pan, add the reserved marinade, stock and wine. Bring the liquid to the boil and simmer, covered, for 1¼ hours. Cook, uncovered, for 15 minutes, or until the sauce is syrupy and the meat is tender. Serve with steamed rice and garnish with extra sliced spring onions.

SERVES 4

Roast peppered beef with onions and potatoes

1 kg (2 lb 4 oz) piece sirloin (striploin) roast
2 tablespoons freshly ground black peppercorns
1 large red onion
4 large roasting potatoes
40 g (1½ oz) butter, cut into small pieces
3 tablespoons beef stock
3 tablespoons red wine

Preheat the oven to 180°C (350°F/Gas 4). Trim the excess fat from the beef, leaving a thin layer. Press the pepper all over the beef.

Cut the onion and potatoes into 5 mm (¼ inch) thick slices and place in a roasting tin. Sit the beef on top, fat side up. Dot the pieces of butter all over the beef and potatoes. Pour in the stock and wine and bake for 35–40 minutes for medium–rare, or until cooked to your liking. Remove the beef from the oven and rest for at least 5 minutes before carving.

To serve, divide the onion and potato mixture among four serving plates and top with slices of beef. Spoon on any pan juices and serve with steamed beans.

SERVES 4

Japanese-style
steak salad

750 g (1 lb 10 oz) rump steak
3 teaspoons vegetable oil
3 teaspoons wasabi paste
½ teaspoon dijon mustard
1 teaspoon grated fresh ginger
2 tablespoons rice vinegar
3 tablespoons pickled ginger, plus
  1 tablespoon pickling liquid
2 tablespoons sesame oil
3 tablespoons vegetable oil, extra

100 g (3½ oz) baby English
  spinach leaves
100 g (3½ oz) mizuna or
  watercress, trimmed
4 radishes, thinly sliced
1 Lebanese (short) cucumber,
  peeled and cut into ribbons
  with a vegetable peeler
3 tablespoons sesame seeds,
  toasted

Generously season the steak with salt and pepper. Heat the vegetable oil in a large frying pan or heat a barbecue flat plate to high direct heat. Add the steak and cook for 2–3 minutes on each side, or until browned. Remove from the pan and leave to rest, covered, for 5 minutes.

Put the wasabi paste, mustard, ginger, rice vinegar, pickled ginger, pickling liquid and ½ teaspoon salt in a large bowl and whisk together. Whisk in the sesame and extra vegetable oils, then add the spinach, mizuna, radish and cucumber to the bowl and toss well.

Slice the steak across the grain into thin strips. Divide the salad among four serving plates, top with the beef slices and sprinkle with sesame seeds. Serve immediately.

SERVES 4

Hot and sour lime soup with beef

1 litre (35 fl oz/4 cups) beef stock
2 stems lemongrass, white part
   only, halved
3 garlic cloves, halved
2.5 x 2.5 cm (1 x 1 inch) piece
   fresh ginger, sliced
90 g (3¼ oz) coriander
   (cilantro), leaves and stalks
   separated, leaves chopped,
   a few reserved for garnish
4 spring onions (scallions), thinly
   sliced on the diagonal

2 strips lime zest, each 1.5 x 4 cm
   (⅝ x 1½ inch)
2 star anise
3 small red chillies, seeded and
   finely chopped
500 g (1 lb 2 oz) fillet steak,
   trimmed and thinly sliced
   across the grain
2 tablespoons fish sauce
1 tablespoon grated palm sugar
   (jaggery) or soft brown sugar
2–3 tablespoons lime juice

Put the stock, lemongrass, garlic, ginger, coriander stalks, 2 spring onions, the lime zest, star anise, 1 teaspoon of the chopped chilli and 1 litre (35 fl oz/4 cups) water in a saucepan. Bring to the boil and simmer, covered, for 25 minutes. Strain and return the liquid to the pan.

Heat a chargrill pan until very hot. Brush lightly with oil and sear the steak on both sides until browned on the outside, but very rare in the centre.

Reheat the soup, adding the fish sauce and sugar. Season. Add the lime juice to taste — you should achieve a hot and sour flavour.

Add the remaining spring onion and the chopped coriander leaves to the soup. Place the beef in the centre of four deep serving bowls. Pour the soup over the top and garnish with the remaining chilli and coriander leaves.

SERVES 4

Balsamic roasted veal cutlets with red onion

1½ tablespoons olive oil
8 veal cutlets
4 garlic cloves, unpeeled
1 red onion, cut into thin wedges
1 tablespoon chopped rosemary
250 g (9 oz) cherry tomatoes
3 tablespoons balsamic vinegar
2 teaspoons soft brown sugar
2 tablespoons chopped flat-leaf (Italian) parsley

Preheat the oven to 200°C (400°F/Gas 6). Heat the oil in a large frying pan over medium heat. Cook the cutlets in batches for 4 minutes on both sides, or until nicely browned all over.

Arrange the cutlets in a single layer in a large, shallow-sided roasting tin. Add the garlic, onion, rosemary, tomatoes, vinegar and sugar. Season with salt and pepper. Cover tightly with foil and roast for 15 minutes. Remove the foil and roast for another 10–15 minutes, depending on the thickness of the veal cutlets.

Transfer the cutlets, garlic, onion and tomatoes to serving plates. Stir the pan juices and spoon over the top. Sprinkle with the chopped parsley and serve immediately. Delicious with a creamy garlic mash and a tossed green salad.

SERVES 4

Chilli beef burgers

500 g (1 lb 2 oz) minced ground)
beef
6 red Asian shallots, finely
chopped
3 tablespoons crisp fried onion
flakes (see Note)
3 garlic cloves, finely chopped
2 long red chillies, seeded and
finely chopped
4 tablespoons finely chopped
coriander (cilantro) leaves
(include some stems)

2–2½ tablespoons chilli garlic
sauce (see Note)
1 egg, lightly beaten
165 g (5¾ oz/2 cups) fresh
breadcrumbs
olive oil, for brushing
1 loaf pide (Turkish/flat bread),
cut into 4 pieces, then halved
through the middle
3 handfuls mignonette or
green oak lettuce leaves

To make the beef patties, put the beef, shallots, onion flakes, garlic, chilli, coriander, chilli garlic sauce, egg, breadcrumbs and 1½ teaspoons of salt in a large bowl and knead well with your hands until the ingredients are thoroughly combined. Cover the bowl and refrigerate for 2 hours.

Using wet hands, divide the beef mixture into four equal portions, roll each portion into a ball, then flatten it slightly to form patties. Heat a barbecue chargrill plate or flat plate to medium direct heat. Brush the patties lightly with oil and cook for about 5 minutes on each side, or until they are browned and cooked through. A few minutes before the patties are done, toast the bread, cut side down, on the chargrill plate for 1–2 minutes, or until it is marked and golden.

Divide the lettuce among four of the toasted bread slices. Add a patty, season, then top with the remaining bread. Delicious served with pineapple mint salsa.

SERVES 4

NOTE: Buy crisp fried onion flakes and chilli garlic sauce from Asian food stores.

Steak and kidney pie

1.5 kg (3 lb 5 oz) chuck steak,
    trimmed and cut into 2 cm
    (¾ inch) cubes
1 ox kidney (500 g/1 lb 2 oz),
    trimmed and cut into 2 cm
    (¾ inch) cubes
60 g (2¼ oz/½ cup) plain
    (all-purpose) flour, seasoned
2 tablespoons olive oil
2 onions, chopped
125 g (4½ oz) button
    mushrooms, quartered

40 g (1½ oz) butter
250 ml (9 fl oz/1 cup) beef or
    veal stock
185 ml (6 fl oz/¾ cup) stout
2 tablespoons worcestershire
    sauce
1 tablespoon anchovy essence
1 tablespoon chopped flat-leaf
    (Italian) parsley
milk, for brushing
600 g (1 lb 5 oz) puff pastry
1 egg, lightly beaten

Toss the steak and kidney pieces through the flour and shake off any excess.

Heat the oil in a large saucepan over medium heat, add the onion and cook for
5 minutes. Add the mushrooms and cook for 5 minutes. Remove from the pan.
Melt one-third of the butter in the pan, add one-third of the beef and kidney and
cook over medium heat, turning occasionally, for 5 minutes, or until browned.
Remove and repeat twice. Return all the meat to the pan, add the stock and stout,
stir and bring slowly to boil. Reduce the heat and simmer for 2 hours. Remove from
the heat, leave to cool, then add the onion and mushrooms, worcestershire sauce,
anchovy essence and parsley. Preheat the oven to 180°C (350°F/Gas 4).

Scoop the filling into a 20 cm (8 inch) ceramic pie dish. Roll out the pastry between
two sheets of baking paper to fit the top of the pie dish. Moisten the rim of the dish
with a little milk and place the pastry over the filling. Press firmly into place and
brush with egg. Bake for 40–45 minutes, or until golden. Serve with a tossed green
salad or steamed vegetables.

SERVES 6

Musaman beef curry

1 tablespoon tamarind pulp
2 tablespoons oil
750 g (1 lb 10 oz) chuck steak, trimmed
    and cut into 3 cm (1¼ inch) cubes
500 ml (17 fl oz/2 cups) coconut milk
4 cardamom pods, bruised
500 ml (17 fl oz/2 cups) coconut cream
2–3 tablespoons Musaman curry paste
2 tablespoons fish sauce
8 baby onions, peeled
8 small new potatoes, peeled
2 tablespoons grated palm sugar (jaggery)
    or soft brown sugar
80 g (2¾ oz/½ cup) unsalted peanuts,
    roasted and ground

Combine the tamarind pulp and 125 ml (4 fl oz/½ cup) boiling water in a small bowl and set aside to cool. Mash the pulp with your fingertips to dissolve, then strain, reserving the liquid.

Heat a wok to hot, add the oil and swirl to coat the side. Add the beef in batches and cook over high heat for 5 minutes per batch, or until browned. Reduce the heat, add the coconut milk and cardamom pods, and simmer for 1 hour, or until the beef is tender. Remove the beef, then strain and reserve the cooking liquid.

Heat the coconut cream in the wok and stir in 2–3 tablespoons of the curry paste. Cook for 10 minutes, or until it 'cracks' — that is, the oil separates from the cream. Add the fish sauce, onions, potatoes, beef mixture, sugar, peanuts, tamarind water and the reserved liquid. Simmer for 25–30 minutes. Serve with steamed rice.

SERVES 4

Chilli con carne

2 teaspoons ground cumin
½ teaspoon ground allspice
1–2 teaspoons chilli powder
1 teaspoon paprika
1 tablespoon oil
1 large onion, finely chopped
2 garlic cloves, crushed
2 small red chillies, seeded and finely chopped
500 g (1 lb 2 oz) minced (ground) beef
400 g (14 oz) tin whole tomatoes
2 tablespoons tomato paste (concentrated purée)
425 g (15 oz) tin red kidney beans, drained and rinsed
250 ml (9 fl oz/1 cup) beef stock
1 tablespoon chopped oregano
1 teaspoon sugar

Heat a small frying pan over medium heat and dry-fry the cumin, allspice, chilli and paprika for 1 minute, or until fragrant. Remove from the pan.

Heat the oil in a large saucepan over medium heat and cook the onion for 2–3 minutes, or until soft. Add the garlic and chilli and cook for 1 minute. Add the mince and cook over high heat for 4–5 minutes, or until the meat is browned, breaking up any lumps with a fork.

Add the tomatoes, tomato paste, kidney beans, stock, oregano, sugar and spices. Reduce the heat and simmer, stirring occasionally and gently breaking up the tomatoes, for 1 hour, or until reduced and thickened. Season with salt and black pepper. Delicious served with tortillas and guacamole.

SERVES 4

Teppanyaki

350 g (12 oz) fillet steak
assorted vegetables, such as green beans,
    slender eggplant (aubergine), shiitake
    mushrooms, red or green capsicum (pepper),
    spring onions (scallions)
12 prawns (shrimp), peeled and deveined,
    with tails intact
3 tablespoons oil
soy sauce, to serve

Slice the meat very thinly — this will be easier if you freeze it for 30 minutes first, then use a sharp knife. Place the meat slices in a single layer on a large serving platter and season well with salt and pepper.

Cut the vegetables into long, thin strips, then arrange them in separate bundles on a plate. Arrange the prawns on a third plate.

The idea with teppanyaki is to cook the meal at the table on a very hot electric grill or frying pan. Lightly brush the pan with the oil. Quickly fry about one-quarter of the meat, searing on both sides, and then push it over to the edge of the pan while you cook about one-quarter of the vegetables and prawns. Serve a small portion of the meat, vegetables and prawns to the diners, who dip the food into soy sauce. Repeat the process with the remaining meat, vegetables and prawns, cooking in batches as extra helpings are required. Serve with rice.

SERVES 4

Thai beef and pumpkin curry

2 tablespoons oil
750 g (1 lb 10 oz) blade steak, thinly sliced (see Note)
4 tablespoons Musaman curry paste
2 garlic cloves, finely chopped
1 onion, sliced lengthways
6 curry leaves, torn
750 ml (26 fl oz/3 cups) coconut milk

450 g (1 lb) butternut pumpkin (squash), roughly diced
2 tablespoons chopped unsalted peanuts
1 tablespoon grated palm sugar (jaggery) or soft brown sugar
2 tablespoons tamarind purée
2 tablespoons fish sauce
curry leaves, to garnish

Heat a wok to hot, add the oil and swirl to coat the side. Add the meat in batches and cook for 5 minutes, or until browned. Remove the meat from the wok.

Add the curry paste, garlic, onion and curry leaves to the wok, and stir to coat. Return the meat to the wok and cook, stirring, over medium heat for 2 minutes. Add the coconut milk, then reduce the heat and simmer for 45 minutes. Add the diced pumpkin and simmer for 25–30 minutes, or until the meat and vegetables are tender and the sauce has thickened.

Stir in the peanuts, sugar, tamarind purée and fish sauce, and simmer for 1 minute. Garnish with curry leaves. Serve with pickled vegetables and rice.

SERVES 6

NOTE: Cut the meat into 2 x 5 x 5 cm (¾ x 2 x 2 inch) pieces, then cut across the grain at a 45° angle into 5 mm (¼ inch) thick slices.

Steak and rocket baguette

3 tablespoons olive oil, plus extra, for frying
1 red onion, sliced
1 teaspoon soft brown sugar
2 teaspoons balsamic vinegar
1 teaspoon thyme
1 tablespoon dijon mustard
3 tablespoons mayonnaise
100 g (3½ oz) rocket (arugula) leaves
500 g (1 lb 2 oz) beef fillet, cut into 4 thin slices
1 thick baguette
2 tomatoes, sliced

Heat 2 tablespoons of the oil in a small saucepan. Add the onion and cook slowly, with the lid on, stirring occasionally, until the onion is soft but not brown. Remove the lid, add the sugar and vinegar and cook for a further 10 minutes, or until the onion is soft and just browned. Take the pan off the stove and stir in the thyme.

Meanwhile, combine the mustard and mayonnaise in a small bowl. Drizzle the rocket with the remaining olive oil and season with salt and pepper.

Heat 1 tablespoon of the extra oil in a frying pan over high heat and cook the steaks for 2 minutes on each side, adding more oil if necessary. Season.

Cut the baguette into four even pieces along the length, then slice each piece in half through the middle.

To serve, put out the bread, along with separate bowls containing the onion, mustardy mayonnaise, rocket, steak and tomato. Let everyone make their own baguette so they can get the perfect mix of all the flavours.

SERVES 4

Beef and bamboo shoot stir-fry

3 tablespoons oil
400 g (14 oz) rump steak, trimmed and thinly sliced
    across the grain
225 g (8 oz) tin sliced bamboo shoots, drained and rinsed
3 garlic cloves, crushed with ¼ teaspoon salt
2 tablespoons fish sauce
8 spring onions (scallions), cut into 4 cm (1½ inch)
    lengths on the diagonal
3 tablespoons sesame seeds, toasted

Heat a wok to hot, add 2 tablespoons of the oil and swirl to coat the side. Add the beef in two batches and stir-fry for 1 minute, or until it starts to turn pink. Remove and set aside.

Add an extra tablespoon of oil if necessary, then stir-fry the bamboo shoots for 3 minutes, or until starting to brown. Add the garlic, fish sauce and ¼ teaspoon salt and stir-fry for 2–3 minutes. Add the spring onion and stir-fry for 1 minute, or until starting to wilt. Return the beef to the wok, stir quickly and cook for 1 minute until heated through. Remove from the heat, toss with the sesame seeds and serve with steamed rice.

SERVES 4

Asian-flavoured
beef stew

2 tablespoons olive oil
1 kg (2 lb 4 oz) chuck steak,
   trimmed and cut into 3 cm
   (1¼ inch) cubes
1 large red onion, thickly sliced
3 garlic cloves, crushed
3 tablespoons tomato paste
   (concentrated purée)
250 ml (9 fl oz/1 cup) red wine
500 ml (17 fl oz/2 cups) beef stock

2 bay leaves, crushed
3 x 1.5 cm (⅝ inch) wide strips
   orange zest
1 star anise
1 teaspoon sichuan peppercorns
1 teaspoon chopped thyme
1 tablespoon chopped rosemary
3 tablespoons chopped coriander
   (cilantro) leaves

Heat 1 tablespoon of the oil in a large saucepan, add the beef and cook in batches over medium heat for 2 minutes, or until browned. Remove from the pan.

Heat the remaining oil in the pan, add the onion and garlic and cook for about 5 minutes. Add the tomato paste, cook for 3 minutes, then stir in the wine and cook for a further 2 minutes.

Return all the meat to the pan and add the stock, bay leaves, orange zest, star anise, sichuan peppercorns, thyme and rosemary. Reduce the heat to low and simmer, covered, for 1½–2 hours, or until tender. Remove the bay leaves and zest. Stir in most of the coriander. Serve with steamed rice, garnished with the remainder of the coriander.

SERVES 4

Veal scaloppine with white wine and parsley

4 x 175 g (6 oz) veal escalopes
30 g (1 oz) butter
3 tablespoons dry white wine or dry Marsala
100 ml (3½ fl oz) thick (double/heavy) cream
1 tablespoon wholegrain mustard
2 tablespoons chopped flat-leaf (Italian) parsley

Place the veal between two sheets of baking paper and pound with a meat mallet or rolling pin until they are 5 mm (¼ inch) thick. Heat the butter in a frying pan and cook the escalopes in batches for 1 minute on each side, or until just cooked. Remove and cover.

Add the wine to the pan, bring to the boil and cook for 1–2 minutes, or until reduced by half. Then add the cream, bring to the boil and reduce by half again. Stir in the mustard and 1 tablespoon parsley until just combined. Return the veal to the pan to warm through and coat in the sauce. Serve the veal with a little sauce and sprinkle with the remaining parsley. Serve with potatoes and a green salad, if desired.

SERVES 4

lamb

Stir-fried lamb with mint and chilli

2 tablespoons oil
750 g (1 lb 10 oz) lamb loin fillet,
    thinly sliced across the grain
4 garlic cloves, finely chopped
1 small red onion, cut into wedges
2 small red chillies, thinly sliced
4 tablespoons oyster sauce
2½ tablespoons fish sauce
1½ teaspoons sugar
50 g (1¾ oz) mint, half chopped,
    the rest left whole

Heat a wok to hot, add 1 tablespoon of the oil and swirl to coat the side. Add the lamb and garlic in batches and stir-fry for 1–2 minutes, or until the lamb is almost cooked.

Heat the remaining oil in the wok, add the onion and stir-fry for 2 minutes, or until the onion is soft.

Return all the lamb to the wok. Stir in the chilli, oyster sauce, fish sauce, sugar and the chopped mint and cook for another 1–2 minutes. Remove the wok from the heat, fold in the whole mint leaves and serve with steamed rice.

SERVES 4

Lamb backstraps with spiced lentils and mint raita

125 g (4½ oz/½ cup) plain
    yoghurt
2 tablespoons finely chopped
    mint
1 tablespoon garam masala
3 teaspoons ground cumin
½ teaspoon chilli powder

4 tablespoons oil
4 x 150 g (5½ oz) lamb
    backstraps or loin fillets
2 teaspoons grated fresh ginger
1 teaspoon ground turmeric
2 x 425 g (15 oz) tins lentils,
    drained and rinsed

To make the raita, combine the yoghurt and half the mint in a small non-metallic bowl. Cover and set aside.

Dry-fry the garam masala in a frying pan over medium heat for 1 minute, or until fragrant. Remove, then dry-fry the cumin. Combine 2 teaspoons each of the garam masala and cumin, the chilli and 2 tablespoons of the oil. Put the lamb in a non-metallic dish. Brush with the spiced oil, cover and marinate for 10 minutes, or overnight if time permits.

Meanwhile, heat 1 tablespoon of the remaining oil in a saucepan. Add the ginger, turmeric and remaining cumin and cook for 30 seconds, or until fragrant. Add the lentils and stir until heated through. Reduce the heat to low, add the remaining garam masala and season with salt. Cover and cook for 5 minutes, adding 3 tablespoons water if the lentils start to stick. Before serving, stir in the remaining mint.

Heat a large frying pan over medium–high heat and add the remaining oil. Cook the backstraps for 3–4 minutes on each side for medium–rare, or until cooked to your liking. Leave for several minutes, then cut into 1 cm (½ inch) thick slices. Place some lentils on a plate, arrange the lamb slices on top and serve with mint raita.

SERVES 4

Lamb kefta

1 kg (2 lb 4 oz) minced (ground) lamb
1 onion, finely chopped
2 garlic cloves, finely chopped
2 tablespoons finely chopped flat-leaf (Italian) parsley
2 tablespoons finely chopped coriander (cilantro) leaves
½ teaspoon cayenne pepper
½ teaspoon ground allspice
½ teaspoon ground ginger
½ teaspoon ground cardamom
1 teaspoon ground cumin
1 teaspoon paprika

Sauce

2 tablespoons olive oil
1 onion, finely chopped
2 garlic cloves, finely chopped
2 teaspoons ground cumin
½ teaspoon ground cinnamon
1 teaspoon paprika
2 x 400 g (14 oz) tins chopped tomatoes
2 teaspoons harissa
4 tablespoons chopped coriander (cilantro) leaves

Preheat the oven to 180°C (350°F/Gas 4). Lightly grease two baking trays. Put the lamb, onion, garlic, herbs and spices in a bowl and mix well. Season with salt and freshly ground black pepper. Roll tablespoons of the mixture into balls and place on the trays. Bake for 18–20 minutes, or until nicely browned.

Meanwhile, to make the sauce, heat the oil in a large saucepan, add the onion and cook over medium heat for 5 minutes, or until soft. Add the garlic and spices and cook for 1 minute, or until fragrant. Stir in the tomato and harissa and bring to the boil. Reduce the heat and simmer for 20 minutes, then add the meatballs and simmer for 10 minutes, or until cooked through. Stir in the coriander, season well with salt and pepper and serve with some pide (Turkish/flat bread).

SERVES 4

Spicy sausages with harissa and couscous

280 g (10 oz/1½ cups) instant couscous
40 g (1½ oz) butter
2 teaspoons harissa
3 tablespoons olive oil
2 tablespoons lemon juice
1½ tablespoons grated lemon zest
2 tablespoons flat-leaf (Italian) parsley, chopped
150 g (5½ oz) chargrilled red capsicum (pepper), sliced
4 tablespoons raisins
12 merguez or other spicy lamb sausages (see Note)
thick plain yoghurt, to serve

Place the couscous in a heatproof bowl with 500 ml (17 fl oz/2 cups) boiling water and the butter. Cover and leave for 5 minutes.

Preheat the grill (broiler). Stir the harissa, olive oil, lemon juice and zest together until well mixed. Add the parsley, capsicum and raisins and leave everything to marinate briefly.

Grill (broil) the sausages for 8 minutes, turning them so they brown on all sides.

Meanwhile, take the lid off the couscous, stir well with a fork to separate the grains, then stir in the harissa mixture.

Serve a mound of couscous with the sausages sliced over it and topped with a large dollop of yoghurt.

SERVES 4

NOTE: Merguez sausages are spicy sausages that are popular in North Africa.

Spring onion lamb

1 tablespoon Chinese rice wine
3 tablespoons soy sauce
½ teaspoon white pepper
600 g (1 lb 5 oz) lamb
   backstraps or loin fillets,
   thinly sliced across the grain
2 tablespoons vegetable oil
750 g (1 lb 10 oz) choy sum, cut
   into 10 cm (4 inch) lengths

3 garlic cloves, crushed
6 spring onions (scallions), cut
   on the diagonal into 4 cm
   (1½ inch) lengths
1 tablespoon Chinese black
   vinegar
1 teaspoon sesame oil

Combine the rice wine, 1 tablespoon of the soy sauce, ½ teaspoon salt and the white pepper in a large non-metallic bowl. Add the lamb and coat in the marinade. Cover and marinate for 10 minutes.

Heat a wok to hot, add 2 teaspoons of the vegetable oil and swirl to coat the side. Add the choy sum, stir-fry briefly, then add 1 garlic clove and 1 tablespoon of the remaining soy sauce. Cook for 3 minutes, or until the stalks are cooked but still crisp. Take the wok off the heat, remove the choy sum and keep warm.

Wipe out the wok and heat over high heat, then add 1 tablespoon of the vegetable oil and swirl to coat the side. Add the lamb in batches and stir-fry over high heat for 1–2 minutes, or until browned. Remove from the wok.

Add the rest of the vegetable oil to the wok if necessary. Add the spring onion and remaining garlic and stir-fry for 1–2 minutes. Mix together the vinegar, sesame oil and the remaining soy sauce. Pour into the wok, stirring for 1 minute. Return the lamb to the wok and stir-fry for another minute, or until combined and heated through. Serve immediately with the stir-fried choy sum and some steamed rice.

SERVES 4

Rack of lamb with mustard crust and parsley potatoes

2 x 6-rib racks of lamb, French-trimmed
3 tablespoons oil
165 g (5¾ oz/2 cups) fresh breadcrumbs
3 garlic cloves, chopped
1 teaspoon grated lemon zest

1 large handful flat-leaf (Italian) parsley, finely chopped
2 tablespoons dijon mustard
150 g (5½ oz) unsalted butter, softened
400 g (14 oz) small new potatoes

Preheat the oven to 220°C (425°F/Gas 7). Score the fat side of the racks in a crisscross pattern. Rub 1 tablespoon of the oil over the racks and season well. Heat the remaining oil in a frying pan over medium heat and cook the racks for 5–8 minutes, or until the surface is completely brown. Remove from the pan.

Combine the breadcrumbs, garlic, lemon zest and three-quarters of the parsley. Add the mustard and 100 g (3½ oz) of the butter to form a paste. Firmly press a layer of breadcrumb mixture over the fat side of the racks, then place in a roasting tin. Bake for 25 minutes, or until the breadcrumbs appear brown and crisp and the meat is cooked to medium. For well-done, continue to bake for a further 10 minutes, or until cooked to your liking. If necessary, cover the breadcrumb crust with foil to prevent it burning.

About 25 minutes before the lamb is ready, toss the potatoes with the remaining butter until well coated. Season, then put in a roasting tin. Bake for 20 minutes, or until browned, then remove, sprinkle with the remaining parsley and season. To serve, cut the racks in half using the bones as a guide. Serve with the pan juices, potatoes and a tossed salad.

SERVES 4

Tandoori lamb with tomato and onion salsa

3 tablespoons tandoori paste
250 g (9 oz/1 cup) thick plain yoghurt
1 tablespoon lemon juice
4 x 4-rib racks of lamb

Tomato and onion salsa
6 roma (plum) tomatoes
1 red onion
2 tablespoons lemon juice
1 teaspoon sugar
2 tablespoons olive oil

Mix together the tandoori paste, yoghurt and the lemon juice in a large non-metallic bowl. Trim any excess fat off the racks of lamb, add them to the marinade and turn them so that they are well coated. Cover and marinate in the fridge for at least 4 hours, or overnight if time permits.

To make the tomato and onion salsa, cut the tomatoes into thin wedges, slice the onion very thinly and toss them both with the lemon juice, sugar and olive oil. Season the salsa with salt and lots of ground black pepper.

Preheat a kettle or covered barbecue to medium–high indirect heat. Cook the lamb, covered, for 10 minutes, then turn it, baste with the marinade and cook it for another 8 minutes. Leave it to rest, covered with foil, for 5 minutes. Serve the racks whole or sliced with the tomato salsa. This is delicious with minted potato salad.

SERVES 4

Pan-fried lamb fillets with red wine sauce

1 tablespoon olive oil
4 x 200 g (7 oz) lamb backstraps or loin fillets, trimmed
170 ml (5½ fl oz/⅔ cup) red wine
1 tablespoon redcurrant jelly
2 teaspoons chopped thyme
30 g (1 oz) butter, chilled and cut into cubes

Heat the oil in a large frying pan and cook the lamb fillets over medium–high heat for 4–5 minutes on each side, or until cooked, but still pink inside. Remove from the pan, cover and keep warm.

Add the wine, redcurrant jelly and thyme to the pan and bring to the boil. Boil rapidly for 5 minutes, or until reduced and syrupy. Stir in the butter. To serve, slice the lamb on the diagonal, divide among four plates and spoon some sauce on top. Serve with steamed vegetables.

SERVES 4

Lamb stuffed with olives, feta and oregano

80 g (2¾ oz/½ cup) pitted
   kalamata olives
3 garlic cloves, crushed
100 ml (3½ fl oz) olive oil
800 g (1 lb 12 oz) eye of loin
   (thick end), trimmed

90 g (3¼ oz) feta cheese,
   crumbled
2 tablespoons oregano, finely
   chopped
4 tablespoons lemon juice

Put the olives in a food processor or blender with the garlic and 2 tablespoons of the olive oil and blend until it is smooth. Season with ground black pepper.

Prepare the loin by cutting horizontally most of the way through the piece, starting at one end, leaving a small join at the other end. Open out the lamb so you have a piece half as thick and twice as long as you started with.

Spread the olive and garlic paste in a thin, even layer over the cut surface of the lamb, then crumble the feta over the top and scatter with the oregano. Roll the lamb tightly, starting with one of the long cut edges, and tie the whole length with cooking twine, so that the filling is contained and secure.

Put the lamb into a dish large enough to hold it lying flat and drizzle it with the lemon juice and remaining olive oil, turning to make sure that all of the lamb is well coated. Cover the dish and marinate in the fridge for 3 hours.

Heat a barbecue chargrill plate or flat plate to medium–high direct heat. Season the lamb and cook, turning to brown each side, for 10 minutes, or until cooked to your liking. Remove from the barbecue and let it rest, covered, for 5 minutes. Cut the roll into 5 cm (2 inch) thick pieces on the diagonal and serve with salad.

SERVES 4

Braised lamb shanks in rich tomato sauce

2 tablespoons olive oil
1 large red onion, sliced
4 x 250 g (9 oz) French-trimmed
   lamb shanks
2 garlic cloves, crushed
400 g (14 oz) tin chopped
   tomatoes

125 ml (4 fl oz/½ cup) red wine
2 teaspoons chopped rosemary
150 g (5½ oz/1 cup) instant
   polenta
50 g (1¾ oz) butter
50 g (1¾ oz/½ cup) grated
   parmesan cheese

Preheat the oven to 160°C (315°F/Gas 2–3). Heat the oil in a 4 litre (140 fl oz/16 cup) flameproof casserole dish over medium heat and cook the onion for 3–4 minutes, or until soft and translucent. Add the lamb shanks and cook for 2–3 minutes, or until lightly browned. Add the garlic, tomato and wine, then bring to the boil and cook for 3–4 minutes. Stir in the rosemary. Season with ¼ teaspoon each of salt and freshly ground black pepper.

Cover with a lid, transfer to the oven and cook for 2 hours. Remove the lid, return the dish to the oven and simmer for a further 15 minutes, or until the lamb just starts to fall off the bone. Check periodically that the sauce is not too dry, adding water if necessary.

About 20 minutes before serving, bring 1 litre (35 fl oz/4 cups) water to the boil in a saucepan. Add the polenta in a thin stream, whisking continuously, then reduce the heat to very low. Simmer for 8–10 minutes, or until thick and coming away from the side of the saucepan. Stir in the butter and parmesan. To serve, spoon the polenta onto serving plates, top with the shanks and a little sauce from the casserole over the shanks.

SERVES 4

Slow-cooked lamb shanks and vegetables

3 tablespoons olive oil
8 small French-trimmed lamb
  shanks
3 tablespoons seasoned flour
2 onions, sliced
3 garlic cloves, crushed
1 celery stalk, cut into 2.5 cm
  (1 inch) lengths
2 long thin carrots, cut into 3 cm
  (1¼ inch) chunks
2 parsnips, peeled and cut into
  3 cm (1¼ inch) chunks

250 ml (9 fl oz/1 cup) red wine
750 ml (26 fl oz/3 cups) chicken
  stock
250 ml (9 fl oz/1 cup) tomato
  passata (puréed tomatoes)
1 bay leaf
1 thyme sprig, plus extra, to
  garnish
zest of half an orange (without
  pith), cut into thick strips
1 parsley sprig

Preheat the oven to 160°C (315°F/Gas 2–3). Heat the oil in a large heavy-based flameproof casserole dish, big enough to fit the shanks in a single layer. Lightly dust the shanks with seasoned flour, then brown them in batches on the stovetop. Remove from the dish. Add the onion, reduce the heat and cook for 3 minutes. Stir in the garlic, celery, carrot and parsnip, add the wine and simmer for 1 minute, then return the shanks to the casserole dish. Add the stock, tomato passata, bay leaf, thyme, orange zest and parsley. Cover and bake for 2 hours.

Remove the shanks from the pan and arrange on warm serving plates. Discard the herbs and zest, then spoon the vegetables and gravy over the shanks. Garnish with the thyme sprigs. Serve with soft polenta or mashed potato.

SERVES 4

Madras lamb pilau

3 tablespoons oil
2 onions, thinly sliced
250 g (9 oz/1 cup) plain yoghurt
3 tablespoons Madras curry paste
400 g (14 oz/2 cups) basmati rice, well rinsed
8 large French-trimmed lamb cutlets
4 tablespoons chopped mint
60 g (2¼ oz/½ cup) slivered almonds, lightly toasted

Heat 2 tablespoons of the oil in a large saucepan, add the onion and cook over medium heat for 4–5 minutes, or until soft. Remove half with a slotted spoon, set aside and keep warm. Add 200 g (7 oz) of the yoghurt and 2 tablespoons of the curry paste to the pan. Cook, stirring, for 2 minutes. Stir in the rice until well coated. Pour in 500 ml (17 fl oz/2 cups) water, bring to the boil, then reduce the heat to medium–low and cook for 15–20 minutes, or until all the water has been absorbed and the rice is tender.

Meanwhile, smear the cutlets with the remaining curry paste and marinate for 5 minutes. Heat the remaining oil in a frying pan over high heat, then cook the cutlets for 3–4 minutes on each side, or until cooked to your liking. Remove from the heat, cover with foil and allow to rest.

Combine the remaining yoghurt with 1 tablespoon of the mint.

To serve, stir the remaining mint through the rice, season, then divide among four serving plates. Top with the reserved onion, the lamb and the almonds. Serve with a dollop of the minted yoghurt on the side.

SERVES 4

Lamb tagine

3 garlic cloves, chopped
4 tablespoons olive oil
2 teaspoons ground cumin
1 teaspoon ground ginger
1 teaspoon ground turmeric
1 teaspoon paprika
½ teaspoon ground cinnamon
1.5 kg (3 lb 5 oz) lamb leg or shoulder,
   cut into 2.5 cm (1 inch) cubes
2 onions, thinly sliced
580 ml (20¼ fl oz/2⅓ cups) beef stock
zest of ¼ preserved lemon, rinsed and cut into thin strips
425 g (15 oz) tin chickpeas, drained and rinsed
35 g (1¼ oz) cracked green olives
3 tablespoons chopped coriander (cilantro) leaves

Combine the garlic, 2 tablespoons of the oil and the cumin, ginger, turmeric, paprika, cinnamon, ½ teaspoon ground black pepper and 1 teaspoon salt in a large non-metallic bowl. Add the lamb and coat it in the marinade. Cover and marinate for 1 hour.

Heat the remaining oil in a large saucepan, add the lamb in batches and brown the meat over high heat for 2–3 minutes. Remove from the pan. Add the onion and cook for 2 minutes, return the meat to the pan and add the beef stock. Reduce the heat and simmer, covered, for 1 hour. Add the lemon zest, chickpeas and olives and cook, uncovered, for a further 30 minutes, or until the meat is tender and the sauce reduced and thickened. Stir in the coriander. Serve in bowls with couscous.

SERVES 6–8

Shepherd's pie
with garlic mash

1½ tablespoons oil
1 large onion, finely
    chopped
1 carrot, finely diced
8 garlic cloves, peeled
750 g (1 lb 10 oz) lean minced
    (ground) lamb

375 ml (13 fl oz/1½ cups)
    tomato pasta sauce
300 ml (10½ fl oz) beef stock
800 g (1 lb 12 oz) all-purpose
    potatoes, cut into large
    chunks
30 g (1 oz) butter

Heat the oil in a large saucepan over medium heat. Add the onion and carrot and cook for 5 minutes, or until soft. Crush 2 garlic cloves and sauté with the onion for another minute. Add the lamb and stir well, breaking up any lumps with the back of a wooden spoon. Cook for 5 minutes, or until browned and cooked through. Spoon off any excess fat, then add the tomato pasta sauce and 250 ml (9 fl oz/1 cup) stock. Cover and bring to the boil. Reduce the heat to medium–low and simmer for 25 minutes. Uncover and cook for 20 minutes, or until the sauce thickens. Preheat the oven to 200°C (400°F/Gas 6).

Meanwhile, cook the potato in a saucepan of boiling water with the remaining garlic for 15–20 minutes, or until tender. Drain well, then return to the pan over low heat, stirring to evaporate any excess water. Remove from the heat, add the butter and the remaining stock and mash until smooth. Season.

Transfer the lamb mixture to a 1.5 litre (52 fl oz/6 cup) ovenproof ceramic dish. Spread the mashed potato over the top. Use a fork to swirl the surface. Bake for 40 minutes, or until the top is golden brown. Serve with a salad.

SERVES 4

Sumac-crusted lamb fillets with baba ghanoush

2 tablespoons olive oil
750 g (1 lb 10 oz) small new potatoes
2–3 garlic cloves, crushed
3 tablespoons lemon juice
1 red capsicum (pepper), seeded and quartered lengthways
4 x 200 g (7 oz) lamb backstraps or loin fillets
1 tablespoon sumac or ground cumin
3 tablespoons finely chopped flat-leaf (Italian) parsley
250 g (9 oz) good-quality baba ghanoush

Heat the oil in a saucepan large enough to hold the potatoes in one layer. Add the potatoes and garlic, and cook, turning frequently, for 3–5 minutes. When golden, add the lemon juice and reduce the heat to medium–low. Simmer, covered, for 15–20 minutes, or until tender (stir occasionally to prevent sticking). Remove from the heat and season well.

Meanwhile, lightly oil a barbecue chargrill plate or flat plate and heat to high direct heat. Cook the capsicum, skin side down, for 1–2 minutes, or until the skin starts to blister and turn black. Repeat on the other side. Put in a plastic bag and set aside.

Coat the lamb with sumac or cumin. Cook on the chargrill plate for 4–5 minutes on each side, or until cooked to your liking. Remove from the heat, cover with foil and rest. Remove the skin from the capsicum and slice the quarters into thin strips.

Stir the parsley through the potatoes. Divide the baba ghanoush among four plates. Cut the lamb into 1 cm (½ inch) thick slices on the diagonal and arrange on top of the baba ghanoush with the capsicum. Serve with the potatoes and a green salad.

SERVES 4

Irish stew

20 g (¾ oz) butter
1 tablespoon oil
8 lamb neck chops, trimmed
4 bacon slices, cut into strips
1 teaspoon plain (all-purpose) flour
600 g (1 lb 5 oz) all-purpose potatoes,
  peeled and cut into thick slices
3 carrots, cut into thick slices
1 onion, cut into 16 wedges
1 small leek, white part only, cut into thick slices
150 g (5½ oz) savoy cabbage, thinly sliced
500 ml (17 fl oz/2 cups) beef stock
2 tablespoons finely chopped flat-leaf (Italian) parsley

Heat the butter and oil in a flameproof casserole dish or a large heavy-based saucepan over high heat. Add the chops and cook for 1–2 minutes on each side, or until browned, then remove from the dish. Add the bacon and cook for 2–3 minutes, or until crisp. Remove with a slotted spoon, leaving the drippings in the dish.

Sprinkle the flour into the dish and stir to combine. Remove from the heat and layer half the potato, carrot, onion, leek, cabbage and bacon in the base of the dish. Arrange the chops in a single layer over the bacon and cover with layers of the remaining vegetables and bacon.

Pour in enough of the stock to cover, then bring to the boil over high heat. Reduce the heat, cover, and simmer for 1½ hours, or until the meat is very tender and the sauce is slightly reduced. Season well with salt and freshly ground black pepper and serve sprinkled with the parsley.

SERVES 4

Mediterranean
burgers

1 large red capsicum (pepper)
500 g (1 lb 2 oz) minced
  (ground) lamb
1 egg, lightly beaten
1 small onion, grated
3 garlic cloves, crushed
2 tablespoons pine nuts,
  chopped
1 tablespoon finely chopped
  mint
1 tablespoon finely chopped
  flat-leaf (Italian) parsley

1 teaspoon ground cumin
2 teaspoons chilli sauce
1 tablespoon olive oil
4 large bread rolls
220 g (7¾ oz/1 cup) ready-made
  hummus
100 g (3½ oz) baby rocket
  (arugula) leaves
1 small Lebanese (short)
  cucumber, cut into ribbons
  with a vegetable peeler
chilli sauce, to serve (optional)

Preheat the grill (broiler). Cut the capsicum into large flattish pieces, removing the seeds and membrane. Place, skin side up, under the grill (broiler) until the skin blackens and blisters. Cool in a plastic bag, then peel and cut into thick strips.

Combine the mince, egg, onion, garlic, pine nuts, herbs, cumin and chilli sauce in a large bowl. Mix with your hands and roll into four even-sized balls. Press the balls into large patties about 9 cm (3½ inches) in diameter.

Heat the oil in a large frying pan and cook the patties over medium heat for 6 minutes on each side, or until cooked through, then drain on crumpled paper towels.

Halve the rolls and toast both sides. Spread the cut sides of the rolls with hummus, then lay rocket, roasted capsicum and cucumber ribbons over the base. Place a patty on the salad and top with the other half of the bread. Serve with chilli sauce.

SERVES 4

Skewered lamb
with chilli aïoli

125 ml (4 fl oz/½ cup) olive oil
125 ml (4 fl oz/½ cup) lemon juice
2 garlic cloves, crushed
1 teaspoon cracked black pepper
1 tablespoon dijon mustard
1 tablespoon chopped oregano
1.5 kg (3 lb 5 oz) leg of lamb,
  boned and cut into 3 cm
  (1¼ inch) cubes

Chilli aïoli
2–3 small red chillies, seeded
3 garlic cloves
½ teaspoon ground black
  pepper
3 egg yolks
2 tablespoons lemon juice
200 ml (7 fl oz) olive oil

Combine the olive oil, lemon juice, garlic, pepper, mustard and oregano in a large non-metallic bowl. Add the lamb and coat it in the marinade. Cover and marinate in the fridge for at least 3 hours, or overnight if time permits. Meanwhile, soak 12 wooden skewers in water to prevent scorching.

Lightly oil a barbecue chargrill plate or flat plate and heat it to high direct heat. Drain the lamb, reserving the marinade. Thread the lamb onto the skewers and chargrill until well browned, brushing with the marinade occasionally.

To make the chilli aïoli, chop the chillies and garlic for 30 seconds in a food processor. Add the pepper, egg yolks and 2 teaspoons of lemon juice. With the motor running, slowly pour in the oil in a fine stream. Increase the flow as the aïoli thickens. Add the remaining lemon juice and season to taste with salt. Serve with the skewered lamb.

MAKES 12 SKEWERS

Goulash

100 g (3½ oz) bacon, julienned
1 onion, chopped
2 tomatoes, peeled and chopped
1 garlic clove, chopped
½ teaspoon caraway seeds, lightly crushed
1½ tablespoons sweet paprika, plus extra, to serve
1 kg (2 lb 4 oz) lamb loin fillet, trimmed
   and cut into 2 cm (¾ inch) cubes
1 bay leaf
250 ml (9 fl oz/1 cup) vegetable stock
450 g (1 lb) new potatoes, cut into 2 cm (¾ inch) cubes
100 g (3½ oz/⅔ cup) fresh or frozen peas
3 tablespoons sour cream

Put the bacon in a 4 litre (140 fl oz/16 cup) flameproof casserole dish and cook over medium heat for 4–5 minutes. Add the onion and cook for 2 minutes, then add the tomato and cook for 1 minute.

Stir in the garlic, caraway seeds, paprika, lamb, bay leaf and stock. Bring to the boil, then reduce the heat to low and simmer, covered, for 40 minutes.

Add the potato and cook, uncovered, for 15 minutes, or until tender, then add the peas and cook for a further 5 minutes, or until the peas are tender. Remove the bay leaf. Stir in the sour cream and gently heat, without boiling. Spoon into bowls, sprinkle with paprika and serve with rye bread.

SERVES 6

Roast lamb

2 rosemary sprigs
3 garlic cloves
80 g (2¾ oz) pancetta
2 kg (4 lb 8 oz) leg of lamb, shank bone cut
    off just above the joint, trimmed and tied
1 large onion
125 ml (4 fl oz/½ cup) olive oil
375 ml (13 fl oz/1½ cups) dry white wine

Preheat the oven to 230°C (450°F/Gas 8). Strip the leaves off the rosemary sprigs and chop them with the garlic and pancetta until paste-like. Season with salt and pepper.

With the point of a sharp knife, make incisions about 1 cm (½ inch) deep all over the lamb. Rub the rosemary–garlic paste over the surface of the lamb, pushing it deep into the incisions.

Cut the onion into four thick slices and put them in the centre of a roasting tin. Place the lamb on top and gently pour the olive oil over it. Roast for 15 minutes. Reduce the temperature to 180°C (350°F/Gas 4) and pour in 250 ml (9 fl oz/1 cup) of the wine. Roast for 1½ hours for medium–rare, or until cooked to your liking. Baste a couple of times and add a little water if the juices start to burn in the tin. Transfer the lamb to a carving platter and leave to rest for 10 minutes.

Remove the onion and spoon off the excess fat from the tin. Place the tin over high heat on the stovetop, pour in the remaining wine and cook for 3–4 minutes, or until the sauce reduces and thickens. Taste for seasoning. Slice the lamb and spoon some of the sauce over the top. Serve with roast vegetables.

SERVES 4

Lamb pittas with fresh mint salad

1 kg (2 lb 4 oz) lean minced (ground) lamb
60 g (2¼ oz) finely chopped parsley
25 g (1 oz) mint, finely chopped
1 onion, finely chopped
1 garlic clove, crushed
1 egg
1 teaspoon chilli sauce

4 small wholemeal (whole-wheat) pitta breads
plain yoghurt, optional

Mint salad
3 small vine-ripened tomatoes
1 small red onion, thinly sliced
25 g (1 oz) mint
1 tablespoon olive oil
2 tablespoons lemon juice

Put the lamb, parsley, mint, onion, garlic, egg and chilli sauce in a bowl and mix together with your hands. Shape into eight small patties. Refrigerate for 30 minutes. Preheat the oven to 160°C (315°F/Gas 2–3).

To make the mint salad, slice the tomatoes into thin rings and put in a bowl with the onion, mint, olive oil and lemon juice. Season well. Gently toss to coat.

Wrap the pitta breads in foil and warm in the oven for 5–10 minutes.

Lightly oil a barbecue chargrill plate or flat plate and heat it to high direct heat. Cook the patties for 3 minutes on each side. Do not turn until a nice crust has formed on the base or they will fall apart.

Remove the pitta breads from the oven. Cut the pockets in half, fill each half with some mint salad and a lamb patty. Serve with some plain yoghurt, if desired.

SERVES 4

Lamb kofta curry

500 g (1 lb 2 oz) minced
  (ground) lamb
1 onion, finely chopped
1 garlic clove, finely chopped
1 teaspoon grated fresh ginger
1 small red chilli, finely chopped
1 teaspoon garam masala
1 teaspoon ground coriander
55 g (2 oz/½ cup) ground
  almonds
2 tablespoons chopped coriander
  (cilantro) leaves, to garnish

Sauce
2 teaspoons oil
1 onion, finely chopped
3 tablespoons korma curry paste
400 g (14 oz) tin chopped
  tomatoes
125 g (4½ oz/½ cup) thick
  natural yoghurt
1 teaspoon lemon juice

Combine the lamb, onion, garlic, ginger, chilli, garam masala, ground coriander, ground almonds and 1 teaspoon salt in a bowl. Shape into walnut-sized balls with your hands.

Heat a large non-stick frying pan and cook the koftas in batches until brown on both sides — they don't need to be cooked all the way through at this stage.

To make the sauce, heat the oil in a saucepan over low heat. Add the onion and cook for 8 minutes, or until soft and golden. Add the curry paste and cook until fragrant. Add the tomatoes and simmer for 5 minutes. Stir in the yoghurt (1 tablespoon at a time) and the lemon juice, stirring until combined.

Add the koftas to the tomato sauce. Cook, covered, over low heat for 20 minutes. Serve over steamed rice and garnish with the coriander.

SERVES 4

Lamb with roasted tomatoes

Cucumber dressing
1 tablespoon red wine vinegar
½ Lebanese (short) cucumber, finely diced
100 g (3½ oz) Greek-style yoghurt
2 teaspoons chopped mint
½ teaspoon ground cumin
1 tablespoon olive oil

6 vine-ripened tomatoes
4 garlic cloves, finely chopped
1 tablespoon chopped oregano
1 tablespoon chopped parsley
3 tablespoons olive oil
600 g (1 lb 5 oz) asparagus, trimmed
2 lamb backstraps or loin fillets (about 500 g/1 lb 2 oz)

To make the dressing, combine the vinegar, cucumber, yoghurt, mint, cumin and olive oil in a cup.

Preheat the oven to 180°C (350°F/Gas 4). Cut the tomatoes in half and scoop out the seeds. Combine the garlic, oregano and parsley, and sprinkle into the tomato shells.

Place the tomatoes on a rack in a roasting tin. Drizzle them with 1 tablespoon of the olive oil and roast for 1 hour. Remove from the oven, cut each piece in half again and keep warm. Place the asparagus in the roasting tin, drizzle with another tablespoon of olive oil, season, and roast for 10 minutes.

Meanwhile, heat the remaining oil in a frying pan. Season the lamb well and cook over medium–high heat for 5 minutes on each side, then set aside to rest.

Remove the asparagus from the oven and arrange on a serving plate. Top with the tomato. Slice the lamb on the diagonal and arrange on top of the tomato. Drizzle with the dressing and serve immediately.

SERVES 4

Lamb curry

1 kg (2 lb 4 oz) lamb leg or shoulder,
   cut into 3 cm (1¼ inch) cubes
4 tablespoons thick plain yoghurt
2 onions, chopped
2 green chillies, roughly chopped
2 garlic cloves, crushed
2 cm (¾ inch) piece fresh ginger, grated
4 tablespoons cashews
4 tablespoons korma curry paste
2 tablespoons oil

Put the pieces of lamb in a bowl with half the yoghurt and mix together until the meat is well coated.

Put the onion, chilli, garlic, ginger, cashew nuts and curry paste in a blender, add 4 tablespoons water and process to a smooth paste. If you don't have a blender, finely chop everything before adding the water.

Heat the oil in a flameproof casserole dish over medium heat. Add the blended mixture, season with salt and cook over low heat for 1 minute, or until the liquid evaporates and the sauce thickens. Add the lamb and slowly bring everything to the boil. Cover the casserole tightly, simmer for 1¼ hours, then add the rest of the yoghurt and keep cooking for another 30 minutes, or until the meat is very tender. Stir the meat occasionally to prevent it from sticking to the pan. The sauce should be quite thick. Serve with steamed rice.

SERVES 4

Lamb cutlets with sweet potato and ginger nori butter

125 ml (4 fl oz/½ cup) Japanese
    plum wine (see Note)
2 tablespoons soy sauce
1 teaspoon finely grated fresh
    ginger
2 garlic cloves, crushed
few drops sesame oil
16 lamb cutlets, trimmed

4 x 200 g (7 oz) orange sweet
    potatoes
vegetable oil, for brushing

Ginger nori butter
90 g (3¼ oz) butter, softened
1½ tablespoons very finely
    shredded nori
2 teaspoons grated fresh ginger

Combine the plum wine, soy sauce, ginger, garlic and sesame oil in a large non-metallic dish. Add the cutlets and coat them in the marinade. Cover and marinate in the fridge for 3 hours.

To make the ginger nori butter, mash the ingredients together with some pepper.

Preheat a covered barbecue to medium indirect heat. Brush the sweet potatoes with a little oil and wrap in a double layer of foil. Put them on the barbecue and replace the lid. Roast for 50 minutes, or until they are tender when pierced with a sharp knife, then remove them from the heat and leave the barbecue uncovered.

Drain the marinade into a small saucepan and boil over high heat for 5 minutes, or until reduced. Brush the chargrill plate with a little oil and cook the cutlets for 1 minute, then turn, brush with the marinade and cook for 1 minute for rare, or until cooked to your liking. Remove from the barbecue, brush with the remaining marinade, cover and rest. Serve with the sweet potatoes topped with nori butter.

SERVES 4

NOTE: Japanese plum wine is available from specialist Japanese grocery stores.

Welsh lamb pie

750 g (1 lb 10 oz) lamb leg or
  shoulder, cut into 3 cm
  (1¼ inch) cubes
90 g (3¼ oz/¾ cup) plain
  (all-purpose) flour, seasoned
2 tablespoons olive oil
200 g (7 oz) bacon, finely
  chopped
2 garlic cloves, chopped
4 large leeks, white part only,
  sliced

1 large carrot, chopped
2 large all-purpose potatoes,
  cut into 1 cm (½ inch) cubes
310 ml (10¾ fl oz/1¼ cups) beef
  stock
1 bay leaf
2 teaspoons chopped flat-leaf
  (Italian) parsley
375 g (13 oz) puff pastry
1 egg, lightly beaten

Toss the meat in the seasoned flour and shake off the excess. Heat the oil in a large frying pan over medium heat. Cook the meat in batches for 4–5 minutes, or until well browned, then remove from the pan. Add the bacon and cook for 3 minutes. Add the garlic and leek and cook for about 5 minutes, or until the leek is soft.

Put the meat in a large saucepan, add the leek and bacon, carrot, potato, stock and bay leaf and bring to the boil, then reduce the heat, cover and simmer for 30 minutes. Uncover and simmer for 1 hour, or until the meat is cooked and the liquid has thickened. Season. Remove the bay leaf, stir in the parsley and set aside to cool.

Preheat the oven to 200°C (400°F/Gas 6). Divide the filling among four 375 ml (13 fl oz/1½ cup) pie dishes. Divide the pastry into four and roll each piece out between two sheets of baking paper until large enough to cover the pie. Remove the top sheet of paper and invert the pastry over the filling. Trim the edges and pinch to seal. Cut two slits in the top for steam to escape. Brush with egg and bake for 45 minutes, or until the pastry is crisp and golden. Serve with a salad.

SERVES 6

Lamb shanks with chickpeas

1 tablespoon oil
4 large or 8 small lamb shanks
2 onions, finely chopped
2 garlic cloves, crushed
1 tablespoon harissa
1 cinnamon stick
2 x 400 g (14 oz) tins chopped
    tomatoes

2 x 300 g (10½ oz) tins
    chickpeas, drained and rinsed
90 g (3¼ oz/½ cup) green olives
2 teaspoons finely chopped
    preserved lemon or lemon
    zest
2 tablespoons chopped mint

Heat the oil in a large flameproof casserole dish over medium heat and fry the lamb shanks until they are well browned all over. Add the onion and garlic and fry for about 2 minutes until the onion starts to soften.

Add the harissa, cinnamon and salt and pepper to the casserole, stir everything together, then add the chopped tomato and bring to the boil. If there doesn't seem to be enough liquid (the shanks need to be pretty well covered), add a splash of water. Put the lid on and turn the heat down until the liquid is simmering, then cook for 50 minutes.

Add the chickpeas, olives and lemon to the pan and stir them into the liquid. Season to taste and continue cooking with the lid off for another 20–30 minutes. By this time, the lamb should be very tender and almost falling off the bone. If it isn't, just keep cooking, checking every 5 minutes until it is. Using a big spoon, scoop any orange-coloured oil off the top, then stir in the mint. Serve with extra harissa if you would like the sauce a little hotter.

SERVES 4

Lamb pilaff

1 large eggplant (aubergine),
   cut into 1 cm (½ inch) cubes
125 ml (4 fl oz/½ cup) olive oil
1 large onion, finely chopped
1 teaspoon ground cinnamon
2 teaspoons ground cumin
1 teaspoon ground coriander
300 g (10½ oz/1½ cups) long-
   grain rice
500 ml (17 fl oz/2 cups) chicken
   or vegetable stock

500 g (1 lb 2 oz) minced
   (ground) lamb
½ teaspoon allspice
2 tablespoons olive oil, extra
2 tomatoes, cut into wedges
3 tablespoons toasted pistachios
2 tablespoons currants
2 tablespoons coriander
   (cilantro) leaves, to garnish

Put the eggplant in a colander, sprinkle with salt and leave for 1 hour. Rinse the salt off and squeeze the eggplant dry. Heat 2 tablespoons of the oil in a large, deep frying pan with a lid, add the eggplant and cook over medium heat for about 10 minutes. Drain on crumpled paper towels.

Heat the remaining oil in the pan, add the onion and cook for 4–5 minutes, or until soft. Stir in half each of the cinnamon, cumin and ground coriander. Add the rice and stir to coat, then add the stock and some seasoning and bring to the boil. Reduce the heat and simmer, covered, for 15 minutes.

Put the lamb in a bowl with the allspice and remaining spices. Season, then mix together. Roll into small balls. Heat the extra oil in a frying pan and cook the meatballs in batches over medium heat for 5 minutes. Drain on crumpled paper towels.

Add the tomato to the pan and cook for 3–5 minutes, or until golden. Remove from the pan. Stir the eggplant, nuts, currants and meatballs through the rice. Serve the pilaff with the tomato and coriander.

SERVES 4

Greek peppered lamb salad

300 g (10½ oz) lamb backstraps or loin fillets
1½ tablespoons black pepper
3 vine-ripened tomatoes, cut into 8 wedges
2 Lebanese (short) cucumbers, sliced
150 g (5½ oz) marinated kalamata olives, drained
   (reserving 1½ tablespoons oil)
100 g (3½ oz) feta cheese, cubed
¾ teaspoon dried oregano
1 tablespoon lemon juice
1 tablespoon extra virgin olive oil

Roll the backstraps in the pepper, pressing the pepper on with your fingers. Cover and marinate for 15 minutes.

Put the tomato wedges, cucumber, olives, feta and ½ teaspoon of the dried oregano in a bowl.

Lightly oil a barbecue chargrill plate or flat plate and heat it to high direct heat. Cook the lamb for 2–3 minutes on each side, or until cooked to your liking. Remove the lamb from the barbecue and keep warm.

Whisk the lemon juice, extra virgin olive oil, reserved kalamata oil and the remaining dried oregano together. Season. Pour half the dressing over the salad, toss together and arrange on a serving platter.

Cut the lamb on the diagonal into 1 cm (½ inch) thick slices and arrange on top of the salad. Pour the remaining dressing over the top and serve.

SERVES 4

Moroccan roast lamb with mint couscous

2 tablespoons olive oil
3 teaspoons ground cumin
3 teaspoons ground coriander
3 teaspoons sweet paprika
3 garlic cloves, crushed
1.5 kg (3 lb 5 oz) easy-carve leg of lamb
250 g (9 oz/1⅓ cups) instant couscous
2 tablespoons chopped mint,
    plus extra leaves, to garnish

Preheat the oven to 180°C (350°F/Gas 4). Combine the oil, spices and 2 cloves crushed garlic to form a smooth paste. Season with salt and pepper. Rub a thick coating of the paste all over the lamb. Place on a rack in a roasting tin and roast for 1¼ hours, basting two or three times. Allow to rest in a warm place for 10 minutes.

Meanwhile, place the couscous in a heatproof bowl with 500 ml (17 fl oz/2 cups) boiling water. Stir in the mint, the remaining garlic and ½ teaspoon salt. Cover and leave for 5 minutes, or until all the water has been absorbed, then gently fluff the couscous with a fork.

To serve, carve the lamb into thick slices and place on a bed of couscous. Pour the pan juices into a gravy boat and serve with the lamb. Garnish with mint.

SERVES 4

Chilli lamb cutlets

4 garlic cloves, crushed
1 tablespoon grated fresh ginger
1 teaspoon vegetable oil
1 teaspoon sambal oelek
2 teaspoons ground coriander
2 teaspoons ground cumin
2 tablespoons soy sauce
2 teaspoons sesame oil
2 tablespoons sweet chilli sauce
2 tablespoons lemon juice
12 lamb cutlets

Combine the garlic, ginger, vegetable oil, sambal oelek, coriander, cumin, soy sauce, sesame oil, sweet chilli sauce, lemon juice and salt and freshly ground black pepper in a large non-metallic dish. Add the cutlets and coat them in the marinade. Cover and marinate for 20 minutes.

Lightly oil a barbecue chargrill plate or flat plate and heat it to high direct heat. Cook the cutlets for 3 minutes on each side, or until cooked to your liking. Serve with steamed rice.

SERVES 4

pork

Pork and white bean chilli

1.3 kg (3 lb) pork shoulder, boned, trimmed and cut into
    2 cm (¾ inch) cubes (about 750 g/1 lb 10 oz meat)
2–3 tablespoons oil
1 large onion, diced
3 garlic cloves, finely chopped
1 tablespoon sweet paprika
½ teaspoon chilli powder
2 tinned chipotle peppers or jalapeño chillies, chopped
1 tablespoon ground cumin
400 g (14 oz) tin chopped tomatoes
2 x 400 g (14 oz) tins cannellini beans, drained and rinsed
30 g (1 oz) coriander (cilantro) leaves, roughly chopped
sour cream, to serve
lime wedges, to serve

Season the pork with salt and freshly ground black pepper. Heat 2 tablespoons of the oil in a large flameproof casserole dish over high heat. Add half the pork and cook for 5 minutes, or until browned. Remove from the pan. Repeat with the remaining pork, using more oil if necessary.

Reduce the heat to medium, add the onion and garlic and cook for 3–5 minutes, or until soft. Add the paprika, chilli powder, chipotle peppers and cumin, and cook for 1 minute.

Return the pork to the pan. Add the tomato and 750 ml (26 fl oz/3 cups) water and simmer, partially covered, for 1–1½ hours, or until the pork is very tender. Add the beans and heat through. Boil a little longer to reduce the liquid if necessary. Stir in the coriander and season. Serve with sour cream and lime wedges.

SERVES 4

Italian sausage and vegetable soup

500 g (1 lb 2 oz) Italian pork
  sausages
1 tablespoon olive oil
200 g (7 oz) piece speck, fat
  trimmed and reserved,
  meat diced
1 large onion, chopped
3 garlic cloves, crushed
1 celery stalk, halved and sliced
1 large carrot, cut into 1 cm
  (½ inch) cubes
bouquet garni
1 red chilli, halved lengthways

400 g (14 oz) tin chopped
  tomatoes
1.75 litres (60 fl oz/7 cups)
  chicken stock
300 g (10½ oz) brussels sprouts,
  halved from top to base
300 g (10½ oz) green beans,
  trimmed and cut into 3 cm
  (1¼ inch) lengths
300 g (10½ oz) shelled broad
  (fava) beans, fresh or frozen
2 tablespoons chopped flat-leaf
  (Italian) parsley

Preheat the grill (broiler), then cook the sausages, turning occasionally, for about
10 minutes, or until browned. Remove and cut into 3 cm (1¼ inch) lengths.

Heat the oil in a large saucepan over medium heat. Add the speck and reserved speck
fat and cook for 2–3 minutes, or until golden. Add the onion, garlic, celery and carrot,
reduce the heat to low and cook for 6–8 minutes, or until softened. Discard the remains
of the speck fat.

Stir in the sausage, bouquet garni, chilli and tomato and cook for 5 minutes. Add the
stock, bring to the boil, then reduce the heat and simmer for 1 hour. Add the brussels
sprouts and both beans and simmer for 30 minutes. Discard the bouquet garni, then
stir in the parsley. Season to taste. Divide among four bowls and serve.

SERVES 4

Caramel pork and pumpkin stir-fry

500 g (1 lb 2 oz) pork fillet, thinly sliced
2 garlic cloves, crushed
2–3 tablespoons oil
300 g (10½ oz) butternut pumpkin (squash), cut into 2 x 4 cm (¾ x 1½ inch) pieces about 5 mm (¼ inch) thick
4 tablespoons soft brown sugar
3 tablespoons fish sauce
3 tablespoons rice vinegar
2 tablespoons chopped coriander (cilantro) leaves
1.25 kg (2 lb 12 oz) mixed Asian greens

Combine the pork with the garlic and 2 teaspoons of the oil. Season with salt and plenty of freshly ground black pepper.

Heat a wok to very hot, add 1 tablespoon of the oil and swirl to coat the side. When just starting to smoke, stir-fry the pork in two batches for about 1 minute per batch, or until the meat changes colour. Transfer to a plate. Add the remaining oil to the wok and stir-fry the pumpkin for 4 minutes, or until tender but not falling apart. Remove from the wok and add to the pork.

Combine the sugar, fish sauce, rice vinegar and 125 ml (4 fl oz/½ cup) water in the wok and boil for about 10 minutes, or until syrupy. Return the pork and pumpkin to the wok and stir for 1 minute, or until well coated by the sauce and heated through. Stir in the coriander.

Put the mixed Asian greens in a paper-lined bamboo steamer over a wok or pan of simmering water for 3 minutes, or until wilted. Serve immediately with the stir-fry and some steamed rice.

SERVES 4

Baked Mediterranean pork cutlets

4 large pork loin cutlets, trimmed
2 tablespoons olive oil
2 garlic cloves, finely chopped
1 tablespoon finely chopped rosemary
2 tablespoons thyme
2 tablespoons balsamic vinegar
4 roma (plum) tomatoes, halved lengthways
1 large red capsicum (pepper), cut into 2 cm (¾ inch) thick slices
4 small zucchini (courgettes), trimmed and halved lengthways

Preheat the oven to 220°C (425°F/Gas 7) and lightly grease a roasting tin. Arrange the pork cutlets in a single layer in the tin. Combine the olive oil, garlic, rosemary, thyme and 1 tablespoon of the balsamic vinegar, then spoon half the mixture over the pork cutlets. Season with salt and freshly ground black pepper. Cover and marinate for 20 minutes.

Place 2 tomato halves, cut side down, on each pork cutlet and sprinkle the tomatoes with the remaining balsamic vinegar.

Toss the capsicum and zucchini with the remaining herb mixture, then add to the tin around the cutlets. Bake for 45 minutes, or until cooked through and well browned. Season to taste. Serve the cutlets with the roast vegetables, a green salad and some crusty bread.

SERVES 4

Ramen noodle soup with Chinese barbecued pork

300 g (10½ oz) dried thin ramen egg noodles
1 litre (35 fl oz/4 cups) chicken stock
4 spring onions (scallions), shredded
4 tablespoons soy sauce
400 g (14 oz) Chinese barbecued pork (char siu)
2 small bok choy (pak choy), roughly chopped
sesame oil, for drizzling

Cook the noodles in a large saucepan of boiling salted water for about 4 minutes, or until they are just cooked, stirring once or twice to make sure they are not stuck together. The cooking time will vary depending on the brand of noodles.

Bring the stock to the boil in a saucepan, then add the spring onion and soy sauce. Taste the stock to see if it has enough flavour and, if not, add a little more soy — don't overdo it though as the soup's base should be quite mild in flavour. Turn the heat down to a simmer. Cut the pork into bite-sized shreds or slices (small enough to pick up and eat with chopsticks).

Drain the noodles and divide them among four bowls. Add the bok choy to the chicken stock, stir it in, then divide the stock and vegetables among the four bowls. Arrange the pork on top, then drizzle a little sesame oil onto each — sesame oil has a very strong flavour, so you will only need a couple of drops for each bowl.

SERVES 4

Salsicce with white beans and gremolata

3 tablespoons olive oil
12 salsicce or thick pork sausages, cut into chunks
6 garlic cloves, smashed
250 g (9 oz) chargrilled red or yellow capsicum (pepper)
2 x 400 g (14 oz) tins cannellini beans, drained and rinsed
1½ tablespoons grated lemon zest
3 handfuls chopped parsley
2 tablespoons lemon juice
extra virgin olive oil, for drizzling

Heat the olive oil in a frying pan and cook the chunks of salsicce until they are browned all over and cooked through. Lift them out of the frying pan with a slotted spoon and put them to one side.

Put 3 garlic cloves in the frying pan and cook them over low heat until they are very soft. Cut the capsicum into strips and add them to the pan, along with the beans and salsicce. Stir together and cook for 2 minutes to heat the salsicce through. Season well with salt and pepper.

To make the gremolata, put the remaining 3 garlic cloves and a little salt in a mortar and smash to a paste with the pestle. Mix in the lemon zest and parsley and season with salt and pepper.

Just before serving, stir the gremolata through the beans and then finish the dish with the lemon juice and a drizzle of olive oil.

SERVES 4

Pork chops pizzaiola

4 pork chops
4 tablespoons olive oil
600 g (1 lb 5 oz) ripe tomatoes
3 garlic cloves, crushed
3 basil leaves, torn into pieces
finely chopped parsley, to serve

Using scissors or a knife, cut the pork fat at 5 mm (¼ inch) intervals around the rind. Brush the chops with 1 tablespoon of the olive oil and season well.

Remove the stems from the tomatoes and score a cross in the bottom of each one. Blanch in boiling water for 30 seconds. Transfer to a bowl of cold water, peel the skin away from the cross and chop the tomatoes.

Heat 2 tablespoons of the oil in a saucepan over low heat and add the garlic. Soften without browning for 1–2 minutes, then add the chopped tomatoes and season with salt and freshly ground black pepper. Increase the heat, bring to the boil and cook for 5 minutes until thick. Stir in the basil.

Heat the remaining oil in a large frying pan with a tight-fitting lid. Brown the chops in batches over medium–high heat for 2 minutes on each side. Place in a slightly overlapping row down the centre of the pan and spoon the sauce over the top, covering the chops completely. Cover the pan and cook over low heat for about 5 minutes. Sprinkle with parsley and serve with steamed greens.

SERVES 4

Cypriot pork and coriander stew

1½ tablespoons coriander seeds
800 g (1 lb 12 oz) pork fillet, cut into 2 cm (¾ inch) cubes
1 tablespoon plain (all-purpose) flour
3 tablespoons olive oil
1 large onion, thinly sliced
375 ml (13 fl oz/1½ cups) red wine
250 ml (9 fl oz/1 cup) chicken stock
1 teaspoon sugar
coriander sprigs, to garnish

Crush the coriander seeds in a mortar and pestle. Combine the pork, crushed coriander seeds and ½ teaspoon freshly ground black pepper in a bowl. Cover and marinate overnight in the fridge.

Combine the flour and pork and toss. Heat 2 tablespoons of the oil in a frying pan and cook the pork in batches over high heat for 1–2 minutes, or until browned. Remove from the pan.

Heat the remaining oil in the pan, add the onion and cook over medium heat for 2–3 minutes, or until just golden. Return the meat to the pan, add the wine, stock and sugar, and season with salt and black pepper. Bring to the boil, then reduce the heat and simmer, covered, for 1 hour.

Remove the meat from the pan. Return the pan to the heat and boil the sauce over high heat for 3–5 minutes, or until reduced and slightly thickened. Pour the sauce over the meat and top with the coriander sprigs. Serve with boiled potatoes.

SERVES 4–6

Bucatini with sausage and fennel seed

500 g (1 lb 2 oz) good-quality Italian sausages
2 tablespoons olive oil
3 garlic cloves, chopped
1 teaspoon fennel seeds
½ teaspoon chilli flakes
2 x 400 g (14 oz) tins chopped tomatoes
500 g (1 lb 2 oz) bucatini or other long, thin pasta
1 teaspoon balsamic vinegar
3 tablespoons chopped basil

Heat a frying pan over high heat, add the sausages and cook, turning, for 8–10 minutes, or until well browned and cooked through. Remove, cool slightly and slice on the diagonal into 1 cm (½ inch) thick pieces.

Heat the oil in a saucepan, add the garlic and cook over medium heat for 1 minute. Add the fennel seeds and chilli flakes and cook for a further minute. Stir in the tomato and bring to the boil, then reduce the heat and simmer, covered, for 20 minutes.

Meanwhile, cook the pasta in a large saucepan of boiling water until *al dente*. Drain and return to the pan to keep warm.

Add the sausages to the sauce and cook, uncovered, for 5 minutes to heat through. Stir in the balsamic vinegar and basil. Divide the pasta among four bowls, top with the sauce and serve.

SERVES 4

Fried rice with Chinese barbecued pork

6 spring onions (scallions)
150 g (5½ oz) snow peas (mangetout), trimmed
200 g (7 oz) Chinese barbecued pork (char siu)
3 teaspoons sesame oil
2 eggs, lightly beaten
2 garlic cloves, finely chopped
550 g (1 lb 4 oz/3 cups) cold cooked
    long-grain white rice (see Note)
2 tablespoons soy sauce

Cut the spring onions and snow peas on the diagonal into very thin shreds. Cut the pork into thin slices.

Heat a wok to hot, add 1 teaspoon of the oil and swirl to coat the side. Add the egg and swirl over the base until just set. Turn over and cook for 30 seconds, or until just lightly browned, then remove from the wok. Allow the egg to cool slightly, then roll up and cut into 1 cm (½ inch) thick slices.

While the wok is still very hot, add the remaining oil, then the garlic, spring onion and snow peas and stir-fry for 1–2 minutes, or until slightly soft. Add the pork, rice, soy sauce and strips of omelette and toss until heated through and thoroughly combined — the soy sauce should turn the rice brown. Remove from the heat and serve immediately.

SERVES 4

NOTE: You will need to cook 200 g (7 oz/1 cup) long-grain rice to obtain the correct amount of cooked rice.

Pork loin roast with apple walnut stuffing and roast vegetables

50 g (1¾ oz/½ cup) walnuts, chopped
1 green apple, peeled and cored
½ teaspoon ground cinnamon
2 tablespoons port
1.5 kg (3 lb 5 oz) rindless, boned pork loin

100 ml (3½ fl oz) maple syrup
8 parsnips, sliced thinly lengthways
500 g (1 lb 2 oz) baby carrots
2 tablespoons oil

Preheat the oven to 200°C (400°F/Gas 6) and preheat the grill (broiler). Lightly oil a large roasting tin. Spread the walnuts on a baking tray and place under the grill (broiler) for 2–3 minutes, or until lightly toasted.

To make the stuffing, coarsely grate the apple and squeeze out the excess juice. Combine the apple, cinnamon, walnuts and port and season to taste.

Unroll the pork loin, then spread the stuffing evenly over one-third of the loin lengthways. Re-roll the loin, tie securely and place, seam side down, in the prepared tin. Roast for 20 minutes. Reduce the heat to 180°C (350°F/Gas 4), baste the pork with some maple syrup and roast for a further 30 minutes.

Toss together the parsnip, carrots and oil in a large bowl and season. Add to the roasting tin and roast for a further 30–35 minutes, or until the vegetables are golden and tender. In the last 10 minutes of cooking, baste the pork again with the syrup. Remove the roast pork from the tin, cover with foil and allow to rest for 10 minutes before slicing. Serve with the vegetables and any pan juices.

SERVES 4

Pork chops with apple and red onion chutney

125 g (4½ oz) butter
2 small red onions, sliced
2 Granny Smith apples, peeled and cored,
   then quartered and sliced
¼ teaspoon ground cloves
4 tablespoons honey
4 x 250 g (9 oz) pork loin chops
2 teaspoons oil
½ teaspoon caraway seeds
700 g (1 lb 9 oz) green cabbage, thinly shredded

To make the chutney, melt 50 g (1¾ oz) of the butter in a saucepan, then add the onion, apple, cloves and honey. Simmer, covered, for 10 minutes over low heat. Increase the heat to medium, cover and cook for another 20 minutes, or until the liquid is reduced to a thick chutney. Allow to cool.

Meanwhile, season the chops well on both sides with salt and ground black pepper. Heat the oil and 50 g (1¾ oz) of the butter in a large frying pan and sauté the chops over medium–high heat for 6–8 minutes on each side, or until browned and cooked through. Remove the pan from the heat, leaving the chops to rest for 2 minutes.

While the chops are cooking, melt the remaining butter in a large saucepan, add the caraway seeds and cabbage and cook, covered, over medium–low heat, tossing a few times with tongs, for 12 minutes, or until tender.

To serve, place a pork chop on each plate and serve the cabbage on the side. Top with a spoonful of chutney.

SERVES 4

Sausages and mash with shallot gravy

4 tablespoons olive oil
200 g (7 oz) French shallots, thinly sliced
1 tablespoon plain (all-purpose) flour
125 ml (4 fl oz/½ cup) red wine
375 ml (13 fl oz/1½ cups) beef stock
1 tablespoon dijon mustard
1.5 kg (3 lb 5 oz) boiling potatoes, chopped
150 g (5½ oz) butter
8 thick pork sausages

To make the shallot gravy, heat 2 tablespoons of the oil in a large frying pan over medium heat. Add the French shallots and cook for 5 minutes, stirring often until they soften. Add the flour and cook for 30 seconds. Increase the heat, pour in the wine and stock and bring to the boil. Reduce the heat and simmer for 10 minutes, or until the gravy thickens. Stir in the mustard, then reduce the heat to medium–low and simmer gently until the sausages and mash are ready.

Cook the potatoes in boiling water until tender. Drain, return to the pan and add 1 tablespoon of the olive oil and 120 g (4¼ oz) butter. Mash until smooth, then season with salt and black pepper.

While the potatoes are cooking, prick the sausages with a fork. Heat a large frying pan over medium–high heat, add the remaining oil and the sausages. Cook for 10 minutes, or until cooked through, turning often.

Whisk the remaining butter into the gravy and season. Place a mound of mash on each plate, then top with 2 sausages and some gravy. Serve with green beans.

SERVES 4

Warm pork salad with blue cheese croutons

125 ml (4 fl oz/½ cup) olive oil
1 large garlic clove, crushed
400 g (14 oz) pork fillet, cut into 5 mm
    (¼ inch) thick slices
1 small or ½ large baguette, cut into
    20 x 5 mm (¼ inch) thick slices
100 g (3½ oz) blue cheese, crumbled
2 tablespoons sherry vinegar
½ teaspoon soft brown sugar
150 g (5½ oz) mixed salad leaves

Put the olive oil and garlic in a jar and shake well. Heat 2 teaspoons of the garlic oil in a frying pan, add half the pork and cook for 1 minute on each side. Remove and keep warm. Add another 2 teaspoons of the garlic oil and cook the remaining pork. Remove. Season the pork with salt and freshly ground black pepper.

Preheat the grill (broiler). Lay the bread slices on a baking tray and brush with a little garlic oil on one side. Cook the bread under the grill (broiler) until golden. Turn the bread over, sprinkle with the crumbled blue cheese, then return to the grill and cook until the cheese has melted (this will happen very quickly).

Add the sherry vinegar and sugar to the remaining garlic oil and shake well. Put the salad leaves in a large bowl, add the pork and pour on the salad dressing. Toss well. Place a mound of salad in the middle of four serving plates and arrange five croutons around the edge of each salad. Serve the salad immediately.

SERVES 4

Pork with paprika, potatoes and shallots

1 tablespoon paprika
4 thick pork loin cutlets
2 tablespoons olive oil
3 tablespoons sherry vinegar
¼ teaspoon cayenne pepper
125 ml (4 fl oz/½ cup) tomato passata
    (puréed tomatoes)
400 g (14 oz) all-purpose potatoes,
    cut into 2 cm (¾ inch) cubes
8 French shallots, peeled
200 g (7 oz) rocket (arugula) leaves

Combine the paprika with ¼ teaspoon each of salt and freshly ground black pepper. Sprinkle over both sides of the pork. Heat the oil over medium heat in a deep frying pan large enough to fit the cutlets in a single layer. Cook the cutlets until browned on both sides.

Pour the sherry vinegar into the pan and stir well to scrape up any sediment stuck to the base. Stir in the cayenne pepper, tomato passata and 250 ml (9 fl oz/1 cup) hot water. Bring to the boil, then add the potato and shallots. Reduce the heat, cover and simmer for 30 minutes, or until the sauce has thickened and reduced by half — check the liquid level once or twice, and add a little water if necessary. Season.

To serve, divide the rocket among four serving plates and place a cutlet on top. Spoon the sauce and potatoes over the top.

SERVES 4

Stir-fried hoisin pork and greens with gingered rice

250 g (9 oz/1¼ cups) jasmine rice
500 g (1 lb 2 oz) pork fillets, thinly sliced
1 tablespoon caster (superfine) sugar
2 tablespoons oil
125 ml (4 fl oz/½ cup) white wine vinegar
250 ml (9 fl oz/1 cup) hoisin sauce
2 tablespoons stem ginger in syrup, chopped
1.25 kg (2 lb 12 oz) mixed Asian greens

Rinse the rice and place in a large saucepan. Add 435 ml (15¼ fl oz/1¾ cups) water and bring to the boil. Cover, reduce the heat to very low and cook for 10 minutes. Remove from the heat and leave to stand, covered, for 10 minutes.

Meanwhile, put the pork in a bowl and sprinkle with the sugar. Toss to coat. Heat a wok to hot, add 1 tablespoon of the oil and swirl to coat the side. Add the pork in batches and stir-fry for 3 minutes, or until browned. Remove. Add the vinegar to the wok and boil for 3–5 minutes, or until reduced by two-thirds. Reduce the heat, add the hoisin sauce and 1 tablespoon ginger, and simmer for 5 minutes. Season to taste. Remove from the wok.

Reheat the cleaned wok over high heat, add the remaining oil and swirl to coat. Add the greens and stir-fry for 3 minutes, or until crisp and cooked.

Stir the remaining ginger through the rice, then press into four round teacups or small Asian bowls, smoothing the surface. Unmould the rice onto four serving plates, arrange the pork and greens on the side and drizzle the sauce over the top.

SERVES 4

Roast rack of pork with fig and Marsala sauce

300 g (10½ oz) dried figs, quartered
4 tablespoons dry Marsala
2 teaspoons dijon mustard
125 ml (4 fl oz/½ cup) chicken stock

1.5 kg (3 lb 5 oz) rack of pork, tied
125 ml (4 fl oz/½ cup) oil
1 large red onion, sliced
18 sage leaves

Preheat the oven to 240°C (475°F/Gas 8). Soak the figs, Marsala, mustard and stock. Meanwhile, score the rind of the pork in lines 5 cm (2 inches) apart, brush with 2 tablespoons of the oil and season. Place in a large roasting tin, cook for 15 minutes, then reduce the heat to 200°C (400°F/Gas 6). Add the onion slices to the tin, bake for 40 minutes, then add the fig mixture and bake for a further 30–40 minutes, or until the pork juices run clear when the thickest section is pierced with a skewer.

Meanwhile, heat the remaining oil in a small saucepan over high heat. Add the sage leaves a few at a time for 30 seconds per batch. Remove with a slotted spoon and drain on crumpled paper towels.

Remove the pork and onion pieces from the oven and allow the meat to rest for 5 minutes. Drain the excess fat from the roasting tin. Reduce the sauce on the stovetop for 5 minutes, stirring to scrape up any sediment stuck to the base of the roasting tin.

Slice the pork into portions, pour on the sauce and garnish with the sage leaves. Serve with the onions and some steamed green beans and mashed potato.

SERVES 4

Pork, asparagus and baby corn stir-fry

1 garlic clove, chopped
1 teaspoon grated fresh ginger
2 tablespoons soy sauce
¼ teaspoon ground white pepper
1 tablespoon Chinese rice wine
600 g (1 lb 5 oz) pork fillet, thinly sliced
1 tablespoon vegetable oil
1 teaspoon sesame oil
6 fresh shiitake mushrooms, thinly sliced
150 g (5½ oz) baby corn
100 g (3½ oz) asparagus, trimmed and cut into
   4 cm (1½ inch) lengths on the diagonal
2 tablespoons oyster sauce

Combine the garlic, ginger, soy sauce, pepper and wine in a large non-metallic bowl. Add the pork and coat in the marinade. Marinate for 10 minutes.

Heat a wok to hot, add half the combined oils and swirl to coat the side. Add half the pork mixture and stir-fry for about 2 minutes, or until the pork changes colour. Remove the pork from the wok. Repeat with the remaining oils and pork mixture.

Add the mushrooms, corn and asparagus to the wok and stir-fry for 2 minutes. Return the pork and any juices to the wok and stir in the oyster sauce. Cook, stirring, for another 2 minutes, or until it is evenly heated through. Divide among four plates and serve with steamed rice.

SERVES 4

Italian sausage and lentil stew

3 tablespoons olive oil
850 g (1 lb 14 oz) Italian pork sausages
1 onion, chopped
3 garlic cloves, thinly sliced
1½ tablespoons chopped rosemary
2 x 400 g (14 oz) tins chopped tomatoes
16 juniper berries, lightly crushed
pinch grated nutmeg
1 bay leaf
1 dried chilli, crushed
185 ml (6 fl oz/¾ cup) red wine
95 g (3¼ oz/½ cup) green lentils

Heat the oil in a large saucepan and cook the sausages for 5–10 minutes, until browned. Remove the sausages from the pan and reduce the heat. Add the onion and garlic to the pan and cook gently until the onion is soft.

Stir in the rosemary and then add the tomato and cook gently until reduced to a thick sauce. Add the juniper berries, nutmeg, bay leaf, chilli, wine and 420 ml (14½ fl oz/ 1⅔ cups) water. Bring to the boil, then add the lentils and sausages. Give the stew a good stir, cover the pan and simmer gently for about 40 minutes, or until the lentils are soft. Stir a couple of times to prevent the lentils sticking to the base of the pan. Add a little more water if the lentils are still not cooked. Remove the bay leaf and chilli before serving.

SERVES 4

Goan pork curry

2 teaspoons cumin seeds
2 teaspoons black mustard seeds
1 teaspoon cardamom seeds
1 teaspoon ground turmeric
1 teaspoon ground cinnamon
½ teaspoon black peppercorns
6 whole cloves
5 small dried red chillies
4 tablespoons white vinegar

1 tablespoon soft brown sugar
4 tablespoons oil
1 large onion, chopped
6–8 garlic cloves, crushed
1 tablespoon finely grated fresh
ginger
1.5 kg (3 lb 5 oz) pork leg, cut
into 3 cm (1¼ inch) cubes

Dry-fry the spices and chillies in a large frying pan for 2 minutes, or until fragrant. Put in a spice grinder or small food processor and grind thoroughly. Transfer to a bowl and stir in the vinegar, sugar and 1 teaspoon salt to form a paste.

Heat half the oil in a large saucepan. Add the chopped onion and cook for 5 minutes, or until lightly golden. Put the onion in a small food processor with 2 tablespoons cold water and process until smooth. Stir into the spice paste.

Put the crushed garlic and ginger in a small bowl, mix together well, then stir in 2 tablespoons water to loosen up the mixture.

Heat the remaining oil in the pan over high heat. Add the pork in batches and cook for 8 minutes, or until well browned. Return all the meat to the pan and stir in the garlic and ginger mixture. Add the onion mixture and 250 ml (9 fl oz/1 cup) hot water. Simmer, covered, for 1 hour, or until the pork is tender. Uncover, bring to the boil and cook, stirring frequently, for 10 minutes, or until the sauce reduces and thickens slightly. Serve with steamed rice and pappadums.

SERVES 6

Sweet and sour pork

600 g (1 lb 5 oz) pork loin, cut
    into 3 cm (1¼ inch) cubes
2 eggs
6 tablespoons cornflour
    (cornstarch)
2 tablespoons oil
1 onion, cubed
1 red capsicum (pepper), cubed

2 spring onions (scallions), cut
    into lengths
250 ml (9 fl oz/1 cup) clear rice
    vinegar or white vinegar
4 tablespoons tomato ketchup
220 g (7¾ oz/1 cup) sugar
2 tablespoons oil, extra

Put the pieces of pork and the eggs in a bowl with 4 tablespoons of the cornflour. Stir everything around until the pork is well coated, then tip into a sieve and shake off any excess cornflour.

Heat a wok to very hot, add 1 tablespoon of the oil and swirl to coat the side. Add the onion and cook for 1 minute. Add the capsicum and spring onion and cook for another minute. Add the rice vinegar, tomato ketchup and sugar, turn down the heat and stir everything together until the sugar dissolves. Bring to the boil and simmer for about 3 minutes.

Mix the remaining 2 tablespoons of cornflour with 2 tablespoons water, add it to the sweet-and-sour mixture, then simmer for a minute until the sauce thickens a bit. Pour the sauce into a bowl.

Heat half the remaining oil in a non-stick frying pan over medium heat. As soon as the oil is hot, slide half the pork cubes into the pan and cook them until they are browned and crisp. Remove from pan. Repeat with the remaining oil and pork. Return all the pork to the pan and add the sauce. Reheat everything until the sauce is bubbling. Serve with steamed rice.

SERVES 4

Stir-fried pork with plum sauce and choy sum

600 g (1 lb 5 oz) choy sum, cut
   into 6 cm (2½ inch) lengths
125 ml (4 fl oz/½ cup) vegetable
   oil
1 large onion, sliced
3 garlic cloves, finely chopped
2 teaspoons finely chopped
   fresh ginger
500 g (1 lb 2 oz) pork loin, thinly
   sliced

2 tablespoons cornflour
   (cornstarch), seasoned
3 tablespoons plum sauce
1½ tablespoons soy sauce
1 teaspoon sesame oil
2 tablespoons Chinese rice wine
   or dry sherry

Bring a large saucepan of lightly salted water to the boil, add the choy sum and cook for 2–3 minutes, or until the stems are crisp but still tender. Plunge into iced water to chill completely, then drain.

Heat a wok to hot, add 1 tablespoon of the oil and swirl to coat the side. Add the onion, garlic and ginger and cook over medium heat for 3 minutes, or until softened. Remove from the wok.

Toss the pork in the seasoned cornflour to coat, shaking off any excess. Reheat the wok over high heat, add the remaining oil and swirl to coat. Add the pork in batches and cook for 3 minutes, or until golden on both sides. Remove.

Drain the oil from the wok and return the meat and any juices. Combine the plum sauce, soy sauce, sesame oil and rice wine, and add to the wok. Cook over high heat for 2–3 minutes, then add the choy sum and return the onion mixture to the wok. Cook, stirring, for a further 2 minutes. Serve immediately with steamed rice.

SERVES 4

Pork loin with pickled eggplant

2 x 500 g (1 lb 2 oz) pieces (about 10 cm/4 inches long)
   pork loin fillet
2 tablespoons hoisin sauce
large pinch Chinese five-spice
4 tablespoons vegetable oil
1 eggplant (aubergine), cut into wedges
2 tablespoons soy sauce
2 teaspoons sesame oil
2 tablespoons balsamic vinegar
¼ teaspoon caster (superfine) sugar
2 bok choy (pak choy), quartered

Put the pork in a dish and add the hoisin sauce, five-spice and 1 tablespoon of the vegetable oil. Rub the mixture over the pork and set it to one side. Heat another 2 tablespoons of oil in a non-stick frying pan and add the eggplant. Fry it until it softens and starts to brown, then add the soy sauce, sesame oil, vinegar and sugar and toss everything together for a minute. Tip the eggplant out onto a plate and wipe out the frying pan.

Put the last tablespoon of oil in the frying pan over medium heat. Add the pork and fry it on all sides until it is browned and cooked through. The time this takes will depend on how thick your piece of pork is — when it is cooked, it will feel firm when pressed. Put the eggplant back in the pan to heat through.

Take out the pork and rest for 1–2 minutes. Cook the bok choy in a saucepan with a little boiling water for 1 minute, then drain well. Slice the pork into medallions and serve with the pickled eggplant and bok choy.

SERVES 4

Pork chops with apples and cider

4 thick pork chops
1 tablespoon oil
2 onions, sliced
2 Golden Delicious apples, cored and cut into wedges
2 teaspoons caster (superfine) sugar
10 g (¼ oz) butter
4 tablespoons alcoholic cider
4 tablespoons cream

Using sharp scissors or a knife, cut the pork fat at 5 mm (¼ inch) intervals around the rind of the chops.

Heat the oil in a large non-stick frying pan, add the onion and fry for about 5 minutes, or until soft and just beginning to brown. Tip the onion out onto a plate.

Add the apple wedges to the pan and fry them for 1–2 minutes — they should not break up, but should start to soften and brown. Add the sugar and butter and shake everything around in the pan until the apple starts to caramelize. Transfer the apple to the plate with the onion.

Put the pork chops in the frying pan, add a bit of seasoning and fry them for 4 minutes on each side, or until they are cooked through. Put the onion and apple back in the pan to heat through, then add the cider and bring to a simmer. Once the liquid is bubbling, add the cream and shake the pan so everything mixes together. Let it bubble for a minute, then season well and serve with potatoes and a green salad — watercress goes particularly well.

SERVES 4

Pork and veal terrine

8–10 thin rindless streaky bacon slices
1 tablespoon olive oil
1 onion, chopped
2 garlic cloves, crushed
1 kg (2 lb 4 oz) minced (ground) pork and veal
80 g (2¾ oz/1 cup) fresh breadcrumbs
1 egg, beaten
3 tablespoons brandy
3 teaspoons chopped thyme
3 tablespoons chopped parsley

Preheat the oven to 180°C (350°F/Gas 4). Lightly grease an 11 x 25 cm (4¼ x 10 inch) terrine. Line the terrine with the bacon so that it hangs over the sides.

Heat the oil in a frying pan, add the onion and garlic and cook for 2–3 minutes, or until the onion is soft. Mix the onion with the mince, breadcrumbs, egg, brandy, thyme and parsley in a large bowl. Season. Fry a piece of the mixture to check the seasoning, and adjust if necessary.

Spoon the mixture into the lined terrine, pressing down firmly. Fold the bacon over the top, cover with foil and place in a roasting tin.

Pour enough cold water into the roasting tin to come halfway up the side of the terrine. Bake for 1–1¼ hours, or until the juices run clear when the terrine is pierced with a skewer. Remove the terrine from the water-filled roasting tin and pour off the excess juices. Cover with foil, then put a piece of heavy cardboard, cut to fit, on top of the terrine. Put weights or food tins on top of the cardboard to compress the terrine. Refrigerate overnight, then cut into slices to serve.

SERVES 6

Adobo pork

170 ml (5½ fl oz/⅔ cup) balsamic vinegar
4 tablespoons soy sauce
3 bay leaves
4 garlic cloves, crushed
6 pork loin chops on the bone
2 tablespoons oil
lime wedges

Combine the vinegar, soy sauce, bay leaves, garlic and ½ teaspoon black pepper in a non-metallic dish. Add the pork chops and coat them in the marinade. Cover and marinate in the fridge for at least 3 hours, or overnight if time permits.

Heat a barbecue chargrill plate or flat plate to medium direct heat. Remove the pork from the marinade and pat it dry with paper towels. Brush both sides of the chops with the oil, season and cook for 8 minutes on each side, or until cooked through. Serve with steamed rice and lime wedges. Delicious with grilled mango.

SERVES 6

Ham braised with witlof

1½ tablespoons oil
10 g (¼ oz) butter
4 witlof (chicory/Belgian endive) heads,
    sliced horizontally
8 thick leg ham slices
2 teaspoons soft brown sugar
185 ml (6 fl oz/¾ cup) dry white wine
2 tablespoons chopped parsley

Heat the oil in a large frying pan, add the butter and when it is sizzling, add the witlof, cut side down, and fry for a minute. Add the slices of ham to the pan and fry them briefly on each side, moving the witlof to one side. Add the sugar and wine to the pan, season well and cover with a lid. Cook for about 3 minutes, or until the witlof is soft.

Take the lid off the pan, turn the heat up and let the sauce bubble until it has thickened and gone quite sticky. Stir in the parsley, then serve.

SERVES 4

Sweet pork

850 g (1 lb 14 oz) pork spareribs
125 g (4½ oz/scant 1 cup) grated palm sugar
   (jaggery) or soft brown sugar
4 red Asian shallots, sliced
1 tablespoon fish sauce
1 tablespoon kecap manis
½ teaspoon white pepper
4 tablespoons loosely packed coriander
   (cilantro) leaves

Remove the bone and outer rind from the ribs. Cut into 1 cm (½ inch) thick slices.

Put the sugar in a wok with 2 tablespoons water and stir over low heat until the sugar dissolves. Increase to medium and boil, without stirring, for 5 minutes, or until the sugar turns an even, golden brown. Add the pork and shallots and stir to coat. Add the fish sauce, kecap manis, pepper and 250 ml (9 fl oz/1 cup) warm water. Stir until any hard bits of sugar have melted.

Cover and cook for 10 minutes, stirring occasionally, then cook, uncovered and stirring often, for 20–30 minutes, or until the sauce is sticky and the meat is cooked. Garnish with coriander and serve with steamed rice.

SERVES 4

index

A
adobo pork 191
Asian-flavoured beef stew 70
asparagus
    Chinese beef and asparagus with oyster sauce 22
    pork, asparagus and baby corn stir-fry 175

B
baguette, steak and rocket 66
balsamic roasted veal cutlets with red onion 53
barbecue, rosemary and red wine steaks with vegetables 18
beans
    pork and white bean chilli 140
    salsicce with white beans and gremolata 151
beef
    Asian-flavoured beef stew 70
    barbecued rosemary and red wine steaks with vegetables 18
    beef and bamboo shoot stir-fry 69
    beef and beet borscht 29
    beef bourguignon 34
    beef, stout and potato pie 14

chilli beef burgers 54
chilli con carne 61
Chinese beef and asparagus with oyster sauce 22
Chinese beef and gai larn stir-fry 41
Chinese beef in soy 5
coconut beef curry on turmeric rice 26
eye fillet with blue cheese butter 37
fajitas 13
fillet steak with mixed mushrooms 18
hot and sour lime soup with beef 50
Italian beef casserole with polenta dumplings 21
Japanese-style steak salad 49
Musaman beef curry 58
mustard-crusted scotch fillet with roast vegetables 42
oxtail and vegetable soup 10
roast peppered beef with onions and potatoes 46
silverside with parsley sauce 17
steak with green peppercorn sauce 25
steak and kidney pie 57
steak and rocket baguette 66

teppanyaki 62
Thai beef and pumpkin curry 65
beetroot, beef and beet borscht 29
bucatini with sausage and fennel seed 156
burgers
    chilli beef burgers 54
    Mediterranean burgers 108
butters
    blue cheese butter 37
    ginger nori butter 124

C
caramel pork and pumpkin stir-fry 144
chilli
    chilli beef burgers 54
    chilli con carne 61
    chilli lamb cutlets 136
    fajitas 13
    pork and white bean chilli 140
    skewered lamb with chilli aïoli 111
    stir-fried lamb with mint and chilli 76
Chinese barbecued pork with fried rice 159
    ramen noodle soup with Chinese barbecued pork 148
Chinese beef and asparagus with oyster sauce 22

Chinese beef and gai larn
    stir-fry 41
Chinese beef in soy 5
coconut beef curry on
    turmeric rice 26
curries
    coconut beef curry
        on turmeric rice 26
    Goan pork curry 179
    lamb curry 123
    lamb kofta curry 119
    Madras lamb pilau 99
    Musaman beef curry 58
    Thai beef and pumpkin
        curry 65
Cypriot pork and
    coriander stew 155

E
eye fillet with blue cheese
    butter 37

F
fajitas 13
fried rice with Chinese
    barbecued pork 159

G
ginger nori butter 124
Goan pork curry 179
goulash 112
Greek peppered lamb
    salad 132

H
ham braised with
    witlof 192
hot and sour lime soup
    with beef 50

I
Irish stew 107
Italian beef casserole with
    polenta dumplings 21

Italian sausage and lentil
    stew 176
Italian sausage and
    vegetable soup 143

J
Japanese-style steak
    salad 49

K
kebabs, skewered lamb
    with chilli aïoli 111

L
lamb
    goulash 112
    Greek peppered lamb
        salad 132
    Irish stew 107
    lamb curry 123
    lamb kefta 80
    lamb kofta curry 119
    lamb pilaff 131
    lamb pittas with fresh
        mint salad 116
    lamb stuffed with olives,
        feta and oregano 92
    lamb tagine 100
    Madras lamb pilau 99
    Mediterranean burgers
        108
    rack of lamb with
        mustard crust and
        parsley potatoes 87
    shepherd's pie with
        garlic mash 103
    skewered lamb with
        chilli aïoli 111
    spicy sausages
        with harissa and
        couscous 83
    spring onion lamb 84
    stir-fried lamb with mint
        and chilli 76

tandoori lamb with
    tomato and onion
    salsa 88
Welsh lamb pie 127
lamb backstraps, with
    spiced lentils and mint
    raita 79
lamb cutlets
    chilli lamb cutlets 136
    lamb cutlets with onion
        marmalade 120
    lamb cutlets with sweet
        potato and ginger nori
        butter 124
lamb fillets
    pan-fried lamb fillets
        with red wine
        sauce 91
    sumac-crusted lamb
        fillets with baba
        ghanoush 104
lamb, roast 115
    Moroccan roast lamb
        with mint couscous
        135
lamb shanks
    braised, in rich tomato
        sauce 95
    lamb shanks with
        chickpeas 128
    slow-cooked lamb
        shanks and vegetables
        96
lentils
    Italian sausage and lentil
        stew 176
    lamb backstraps with
        spiced lentils and mint
        raita 79

M
Madras lamb pilau 99
meatballs, lamb kefta 80
Mediterranean burgers 108

Mediterranean pork cutlets, baked 147
Moroccan roast lamb with mint couscous 135
Musaman beef curry 58
mustard
   mustard-crusted scotch fillet with roast vegetables 42
   rack of lamb with mustard crust and parsley potatoes 87

O

oxtail and vegetable soup 10

P

peppered beef, roast, with onions and potatoes 46
peppered lamb salad, Greek 132
pies
   beef, stout and potato pie 14
   steak and kidney pie 57
   Welsh lamb pie 127
pittas, lamb, with fresh mint salad 116
pork
   adobo pork 191
   caramel pork and pumpkin stir-fry 144
   Cypriot pork and coriander stew 155
   fried rice with Chinese barbecued pork 159
   Goan pork curry 179
   Italian sausage and lentil stew 176
   pork, asparagus and baby corn stir-fry 175

pork with paprika, potatoes and shallots 168
pork and veal terrine 188
pork and white bean chilli 140
roast rack of pork with fig and Marsala sauce 172
sausages and mash with shallot gravy 164
stir-fried hoisin pork and greens with gingered rice 171
stir-fried pork with plum sauce and choy sum 183
sweet pork 195
sweet and sour pork 180
warm pork salad with blue cheese croutons 167
pork, Chinese barbecued
fried rice with Chinese barbecued pork 159
ramen noodle soup with Chinese barbecued pork 148
pork chops
   adobo pork 191
   pork chops with apple and red onion chutney 163
   pork chops with apples and cider 187
   pork chops pizzaiola 152
pork cutlets, baked Mediterranean 147
pork loin with pickled eggplant 184
pork loin roast with apple walnut stuffing and roast vegetables 160

pork sausage
   bucatini with sausage and fennel seed 156
   Italian sausage and lentil stew 176
   Italian sausage and vegetable soup 143
   salsicce with white beans and gremolata 151
   sausages and mash with shallot gravy 164
potatoes
   beef, stout and potato pie 14
   Irish stew 107
   pork with paprika, potatoes and shallots 168
   rack of lamb with mustard crust and parsley potatoes 87
   shepherd's pie with garlic mash 103

R

ramen noodle soup with Chinese barbecued pork 148
rosemary and red wine steaks, barbecued, with vegetables 18

S

salads
   Greek peppered lamb salad 132
   Japanese-style steak salad 49
   warm pork salad with blue cheese croutons 167
salsa, tomato and onion 88

salsicce with white beans and gremolata 151
sauce, parsley 17
sausages
    bucatini with sausage and fennel seed 156
    Italian sausage and lentil stew 176
    Italian sausage and vegetable soup 143
    salsicce with white beans and gremolata 151
    sausages and mash with shallot gravy 164
    spicy sausages with harissa and couscous 83
shepherd's pie with garlic mash 103
silverside with parsley sauce 17
skewered lamb with chilli aïoli 111
soup
    beef and beet borscht 29
    goulash 112
    hot and sour lime soup with beef 50
    Italian sausage and vegetable soup 143
    oxtail and vegetable soup 10
    ramen noodle soup with Chinese barbecued pork 148
spicy sausages with harissa and couscous 83
spring onion lamb 84
steak
    barbecued rosemary and red wine steaks with vegetables 18

fillet steak with mixed mushrooms 30
steak with green peppercorn sauce 25
steak and kidney pie 57
steak and rocket baguette 66
steak salad, Japanese-style 49
stews
    Asian-flavoured beef stew 70
    beef bourguignon 34
    Cypriot pork and coriander stew 155
    goulash 112
    Irish stew 107
    Italian beef casserole with polenta dumplings 21
    Italian sausage and lentil stew 176
    lamb tagine 100
stir-fries
    beef and bamboo shoot stir-fry 69
    caramel pork and pumpkin stir-fry 144
    Chinese beef and gai larn stir-fry 41
    pork, asparagus and baby corn stir-fry 175
    stir-fried hoisin pork and greens with gingered rice 171
    stir-fried lamb with mint and chilli 76
    stir-fried pork with plum sauce and choy sum 183
sumac-crusted lamb fillets with baba ghanoush 104

sweet pork 195
sweet and sour pork 180

T
tandoori lamb with tomato and onion salsa 88
teppanyaki 62
terrine, pork and veal 188
Thai beef and pumpkin curry 65
tomato and onion salsa 88

V
veal
    balsamic roasted veal cutlets with red onion 53
    pork and veal terrine 188
    veal parmigiana 38
    veal scaloppine with sage 33
    veal scaloppine with white wine and parsley 73

W
Welsh lamb pie 127

First published in 2009 by Murdoch Books Pty Limited

Murdoch Books Australia
Pier 8/9, 23 Hickson Road
Millers Point NSW 2000
Phone: +61 (0) 2 8220 2000
Fax: +61 (0) 2 8220 2558
www.murdochbooks.com.au

Murdoch Books UK Limited
Erico House, 6th Floor
93–99 Upper Richmond Road,
Putney, London SW15 2TG
Phone: +44 (0) 20 8785 5995
Fax: +44 (0) 20 8785 5985
www.murdochbooks.co.uk

Chief Executive: Juliet Rogers
Publishing Director: Kay Scarlett

Design manager: Vivien Valk
Project manager: Gordana Trifunovic
Editor: Zoë Harpham
Design concept: Alex Frampton
Designer: Susanne Geppert
Production: Alexandra Gonzalez
Recipes developed by the Murdoch Books Test Kitchen

Printed by Sing Cheong Printing Co. Ltd in 2009. PRINTED IN HONG KONG.
National Library of Australia Cataloguing-in-Publication Data
    Meat. Includes index.
    ISBN 978 1 74196 3793 (pbk).
    1. Cookery (Meat) (Series: Test kitchen) 641.36

© Text, design and photography copyright Murdoch Books 2009. All rights reserved.
No part of this publication may be reproduced, stored in a retrieval system or transmitted
in any form or by any means, electronic, mechanical, photocopying, recording or otherwise
without the prior written permission of the publisher.

IMPORTANT: Those who might be at risk from the effects of salmonella poisoning (the
elderly, pregnant women, young children and those suffering from immune deficiency
diseases) should consult their doctor with any concerns about eating raw eggs.

CONVERSION GUIDE: You may find cooking times vary depending on the oven you
are using. For fan-forced ovens, as a general rule, set the oven temperature to 20°C (35°F)
lower than indicated in the recipe. We have used 20 ml (4 teaspoon) tablespoon measures.
If you are using a 15 ml (3 teaspoon) tablespoon, for most recipes the difference will not
be noticeable. However, for recipes using baking powder, gelatine, bicarbonate of soda
(baking soda), small amounts of flour and cornflour (cornstarch), add an extra teaspoon
for each tablespoon specified.